WRITING HANDBOOKS

Ghostwriting

WRITING HANDBOOKS

Ghostwriting

Andrew Crofts

A & C Black • London

First published 2004
A & C Black Publishers Limited
37 Soho Square, London W1D 3QZ
www.acblack.com

ISBN 0–7136–6786–9

A CIP catalogue record for this book is
available from the British Library.

A & C Black uses paper produced with elemental chlorine-free pulp,
harvested from managed sustainable forests.

Typeset in 10.5/12.5pt Sabon
Printed and bound in Great Britain by
Creative Print and Design (Wales), Ebbw Vale

Contents

Introduction

The cult of celebrity has spawned a lucrative niche market for the writer with no ego and limitless discretion. Someone who is content to see the autobiography of the pop star, the footballer or the actor sell by the cartload, knowing that they wrote every word, but who is not going to gnash their teeth in resentment or dish the unpublished dirt drunkenly revealed as the tape recorder, forgotten, spun on.

No, the ghostwriter simply cashes their cheque, files away their transcripts and waits for the next phone call. Not that a ghostwriter's voice-mail is permanently cluttered with messages from soap stars' agents. The calls are just as likely to come from what publishing calls 'the obscures' – unknown people with extraordinary tales to tell, but who can't write them themselves.

Sue Norris, *FT Weekend* magazine

There is nothing new about the craft of ghostwriting; scribes have been doing it ever since the concept of written language was first invented. It happened in similar ways all over the globe. An elderly African chief, whose autobiography I was recently ghosting, remembered how his mother, as one of the few educated women in his town, used to write letters to soldiers on behalf of their wives when the men were away at war. She would also offer to read the replies that the husbands either wrote, or had written for them, but she usually found that the women were more interested in any money that might be enclosed than in hearing news from the front. There has doubtless always been a commercial element to any ghosting job.

Celebrities and their entourages have also been a source of work for ghosts ever since the printing presses started to roll. The Empress Josephine is on record as having hired ghostwriters to tell her story for her, just as those who have access to royal, sporting and showbusiness kiss-and-tell secrets do today.

With the rise of literacy has come a rise in the number of people able to write for themselves, but at the same time there has been an increase in the numbers that want to tell their stories in print and a corresponding increase in the requirements for professionally produced manuscripts. If publishers are inundated with manuscripts begging to be bought, they're going to choose the ones that are presented to the most professional standards. While there may be more people educated enough to write letters and read newspapers than there were in Josephine's day, it's still a long jump from there to writing entire books, or even entire articles. Although they are less often called upon to write personal letters, the ghostwriters of the world have never been as busy as they are today, producing articles on behalf of celebrities or corporate clients, penning autobiographies, speeches, how-to books and even turning other people's ideas for fiction into reality.

In this book I want to explain why I think ghostwriting is an enjoyable and rewarding way to earn a living, and to give some pointers as to how to get the commissions and then bring them to a successful conclusion. I hope you will forgive me if I use some of my own work as examples.

1

Why Become a Ghostwriter?

The Great Gatsby theory

'I was within and without, simultaneously enchanted and repelled by the inexhaustible variety of life.'

F. Scott Fitzgerald in *The Great Gatsby*

When I was 17 and unsure what I wanted to do with my life, a far-sighted schoolteacher gave me a copy of the *The Great Gatsby*. As I read F. Scott Fitzgerald's account of that glamorous world, I decided *that* was who I wanted to be – Jay Gatsby. There was the immense personal fortune, the mysterious past, the magnificent parties, the mansion, the wardrobe full of pink suits – who could ask for anything more?

Now, when I reread the book I find a telling sentence from Fitzgerald about his hero: 'So he invented just the sort of Jay Gatsby that a 17-year-old boy would be likely to invent, and to this conception he was faithful to the end.' No wonder I was hooked.

As I read further on in that first exposure to the story, I gradually realised that the interestingly mysterious past I so envied was about to catch up with my hero; that he was in fact something of a skunk, a vain man with an empty life who was going to come to a very sticky end on an inflatable mattress in his own swimming pool. I decided to revise my plan.

I was still deeply attracted to the idea of getting inside the lives of people like Gatsby, as long as I could be sure that I could walk away before the swimming pool scene. The answer was suddenly obvious. The book was narrated by Nick Carraway, a writer staying in a cottage in the grounds of the mansion. Nick became involved with the dissolute lives of the main characters, uncovered the very stuff of their souls and then went back to the solitary safety of his home to write his story once things turned nasty.

Eureka! That was what being a writer would be about. It would mean dipping into interesting and exciting lives, finding out as much as I wanted before returning to the peace and security of my own garret in order to write the resulting story – whether it be a book, a film script, or an article for the local parish magazine.

At one stage, when Carraway is deeply involved in the convoluted lives of Jay and his wealthy, dissolute friends, Fitzgerald has him writing, 'I was within and without, simultaneously enchanted and repelled by the inexhaustible variety of life.' That, I think, sums up the attraction of ghostwriting. When I chose to write a novel about a ghostwriter (*Maisie's Amazing Maids*), it was because our lives are episodic, just like those of policemen, lawyers and doctors. It is ideal for any dramatic series if the profession of the main character involves different sets of people with each adventure; after all, nearly all television drama series work to the same premise. It is a fascinating way to live if you are someone who enjoys trying out new and different lives, and who is comfortable being a spectator for much of the time.

Finding stories

The greatest problem facing any professional writer is finding a steady supply of ideas and subjects so dazzlingly certain to appeal to the book-buying public that publishers are eager to buy and willing to pay. However, not only are saleable ideas in short supply, it also takes an inordinate amount of time to research any new subject deeply enough to be able to successfully write a book about it. You might spend months, or even years, researching a subject from a number of different sources and still be unable to find a publisher who will offer enough money to make the project viable. As a result the book will either become a labour of love or will never get written at all.

One answer to this apparent 'Catch 22' situation is to collaborate with other people who lack writing skills and experience but have good stories to tell, either as fiction or non-fiction, or who possess all the necessary information to create a book. If these people are also distinguished or celebrated in their own fields, so much the better, since you will be much more likely to catch a publisher's attention if you have a famous name attached to a project.

The man in the white suit

This realisation came to me when I was working as a freelance journalist, interviewing a 'management guru' for a business magazine. He was a flamboyant showman who had created a business for himself training salesmen. Dressed in white suits, travelling in a Rolls Royce (just a hint of the Gatsbys, there), he would hire venues like the Albert Hall and fill them with salesmen eager for tips on how to increase their sales and consequently their incomes. As we reached the end of the interview in one of the drawing rooms of his recently refurbished mansion (another Gatsby touch), he told me that a book publisher had commissioned him to produce a series of 'how-to management titles'.

He'd written books before and was perfectly capable of doing so again, he assured me, except for the fact that his schedule was packed with touring dates, and the sort of money the publisher was offering was not enough to get him out of bed any more. He did, however, still want the books to be written and published because of their promotional value for his business. Nothing adds to a management guru's credibility more than to have penned a best-selling tome or two.

'Why don't you write them for me,' he suggested, 'then I'll get the glory and you'll get the money?'

Since the money on offer from the publisher was more than enough to get a humble scribe out of bed, if not a crowd-pulling management guru, I agreed to the idea. Initially I was a little uncertain, having always assumed that writers had to be totally in charge of the creative writing process, from the first germ of the idea to the final copies reaching the shops; but as work progressed I realised that I had stumbled across the perfect way to gain instant access to the sort of material needed to create books.

Had I myself decided to write a book on 'doubling your sales', I would have had to go round interviewing any number of experts in the business. Then, when I finally approached publishers with the idea, they would – quite rightly – have wanted to know what my qualifications were for writing such a title and how I was planning to promote it, given that I had no track record as a salesman or as an expert in the management field myself. But this way I had all the guru's credibility behind me, not to mention all the material in his head and in his filing cabinets, which I could call on. The publisher was already on board and desperate to receive the words; the hardest part, i.e. the selling of the project, was over; all I had to do was understand the subject and then write the material, which were the two processes I enjoyed the most and the reasons I had chosen the profession of writing in the first place.

It dawned on me then that the world must be full of people who have the material for saleable books in their heads but who lack the time or the inclination to produce the books themselves. They might be celebrities whose notoriety would impress publishers, or ordinary people who had undergone extraordinary experiences. Alternatively, they might be experts in subjects that sections of the reading public wanted to know more about, like my man in the white suit. I realised that if I wanted to spend the rest of my life as a professional writer *and* be able to feed my children, and if I wanted to track down some of the best material around, then offering my services to the world as a ghost would be a very good way of going about it.

The publisher's point of view

As I started to talk to publishers I discovered that in most cases, far from seeing ghostwriters as some sort of second-class citizens, many of them were delighted whenever they discovered that an experienced professional writer was involved in any project.

It's much easier for them to market books by celebrities or established experts than those by unknown writers. The biggest problem that their marketing departments face is making the reading public aware of a book's existence, and in most cases that is down to how much exposure can be obtained for the author. In Britain alone something like 100,000 new titles come out every year. It is virtually impossible to bring the name of an unknown writer to the attention of people who would be interested in what he or she has to say without spending a fortune in advertising, which publishers are always loathe to do until they can be more confident of the likely sales. But someone who is already known to the public immediately has a head start, as potential buyers will recognise them and the media will be more likely to interview them and mention the fact that they've written a book. It's much easier for someone to recommend a book to someone else if the name of the author is famous: trying to remember the name of a first-time author we've read and liked is a struggle for all of us.

Apart from a handful of literary stars, few people buy books because of the names of the authors, and the media have a limited amount of space in which to write about them. But if you write the autobiography of a soap star, controversial politician or sporting hero, the resulting book will be widely written and talked about in the media and the author instantly recognisable to the casual browser in any bookstore. While the famous author is spending several weeks being whisked around all day from breakfast television to late night radio, the ghost can stay comfortably at home and get on with their next project which, with any luck, will be something entirely different.

I ghosted an autobiography of Gillian Taylforth, an excellent actress who was at the time enduring a high-profile persecution in the tabloid media while she was still appearing in *EastEnders*. At the time the book came out there wasn't a radio or television chat show or book programme that didn't want to have her on, and the publishers were able to keep her talking to the public about the book from the moment she woke up on the day of publication to the moment she went to bed. If I had written a biography of her under my own name, the publishers might have been able to lever me into one or two of these slots, but it is unlikely that anyone would have taken much notice, or rushed out to buy the book as a result of listening to me. Far better to leave the promotion of the product to a professional entertainer who knew exactly how to hold the attention of the viewers, listeners and journalists.

Having realised that they want star names (or well-known ones at the very least) attached to as many of their books as possible, publishers will next have to worry about how to get these busy and successful people – whether they are revered academics or popular footballers – to sit still long enough to produce a manuscript to a publishable standard. If they know that the project is in the hands of a reputable and experienced professional ghost they will immediately feel more comfortable. Editors in the modern world are under the most enormous pressure and have far less time to work on manuscripts themselves than they might have done in the past. If they know that the text is likely to arrive by the due date in a more or less finished state, they're much more likely to be willing to pay decent advances and to gear the marketing and sales teams up to give the resulting book their full attention. They do not want to find themselves in the uncomfortable position of having to nag an eminent cabinet minister, Shakespearian actor or international footballer about missed deadlines; they would much rather have the ghost doing that for them.

Avoiding the 'slush pile'

Between the would-be author and the promised land of 'publication' lies a terrible, treacherous marshland known as the 'slush pile'. This is a ghastly, dark and inhospitable place where most people's dreams and aspirations become mired, strangled and suffocated, and eventually sink from sight leaving only despair in their wake. The slush pile seeps into every publisher and agent's office, taking the form of a thick pile of unsolicited manuscripts, synopses and letters of enquiry lying in wait for someone to pick them up and respond with glowing encouragement. These days, due to the ease of word processing and increased literacy, this bog of despair has become so deep it's impossible that anyone will ever get to the bottom of it. If all the publishers and all the agents hired an army of readers to work 24 hours a day, they would still never be able to clear it. Once you have sunk to the bottom of this pit your hopes of ever being noticed pretty much vanish. You have to find a way to stay visible if you want to be noticed.

One way to float to the top is by donning the ghostwriting lifebelt.

If an agent or a publisher can see in the first few lines of the pitch letter that there is a famous or distinguished name attached to the book, and that this will help with the marketing and product distinction, you will immediately receive more attention. If you are an unknown exercise and diet expert, for instance, and you want to write a book on your theories, you may or may not be able to catch someone's attention. If, however, you have a client who is glamorous and constantly on television and you can persuade her to put her household name to the book with you, your chances of being noticed will be instantly transformed. 'Mary Smith's Diet Book' is never going to be as good a potential seller as 'Nicole Kidman's Diet Book, written with Mary Smith'.

Even if you are writing the book for someone who isn't quite as famous as Ms Kidman, there are likely to be promotional angles to the story that wouldn't exist if you were writing it under your own name. If you are a writer and you produce a book on fishing, for example, you will have more difficulty getting the fishing industry journalists to write about it than if you are a well-known professional fisherman and could provide masterclasses for journalists.

Writers who don't have anything with which to catch the attention of eventual readers – and before them, bookshop buyers, the media, publishers and agents – can seldom extract themselves from the slush pile. Ghostwriting is all about hooks and angles, and ways of making the voice of your subject heard above the competitive din.

Increasing the dramatic effect

It's much easier as a writer to make a scene affecting if you are writing it in the first person rather than the third. I would imagine that most of us write our first novels in the first person for exactly this reason.

The following scenes are from a couple of books I wrote for Zana Muhsen, called *Sold* and *A Promise to Nadia*. Imagine how different they would sound if I had been describing them in the third person. I'm not saying it would be impossible, but I don't believe they would be quite as effective.

In this extract from *Sold*, Zana, a 15-year-old Birmingham girl, discovers once she arrives in the Yemen that her father's offer of 'a holiday of a lifetime' is actually something very different.

When we got back from the shops Abdul Khada and I were sitting outside on the platform, talking to the old couple and the children, when Mohammed's younger brother Abdullah arrived up the same path that we had first climbed. I knew there was another boy and I'd been told that he was in a different village about two hours' drive away called Campais. Abdul Khada owned a restaurant in Campais, which was next to the main road out to Sana'a. Abdullah had been helping his father to fix it up in preparation for opening. I'd been shown pictures of the boy before I came out, but I hadn't taken much notice. I knew he was fourteen, but he looked more like ten to me. He was a weak, sickly looking little boy, very thin and pale. The whole family came out of the house to greet him, and his mother took his bag in for him. Ward seemed particularly fond of her second son. Later I was to find out that he had been sickly ever since he was born and that made her specially protective towards him.

'This is my son, Abdullah.' Abdul Khada introduced us, we shook hands, very formally, just as I had with everyone else two days earlier. His handshake seemed weak, and his hand was smaller than mine. We all sat down again outside, and I went on talking to Abdul Khada and the others and took no more notice of Abdullah, apart from being polite. He didn't seem very interesting to me, but I wanted to get on with everyone in the family if possible, and to get to know them. I wanted it to be a good holiday.

As the sun began to go down behind the mountains and the air cooled, we all went inside and sat in my room, still talking. After a while the rest of the family left the room. Abdul Khada sat on the blanket-covered platform, between me and the boy. I was in my favourite place next to the window, which was the coolest spot in the room. The boy was staring at the floor, saying nothing.

Abdul Khada spoke softly and casually to me. 'This is your husband.'

I thought it was a joke. I just looked at him, not sure whether to laugh or not. 'What?' I asked.

'Abdullah is your husband,' he repeated, and I tried to concentrate on the words he was saying, unable to believe that I was hearing them right. My heart was crashing so loudly inside my ribs that I couldn't be sure what I was hearing. I felt short of breath and panic-stricken.

Many of the readers of *Sold* have been girls of a similar age to Zana and her sister, Nadia, and I believe that they are much more able to empathise with her words and thoughts than with those of an older, male writer who had never actually undergone the experiences that the girls were going through.

The following extract is from *A Promise to Nadia*, which I wrote with Zana ten years after we had written *Sold*. By that time *Sold* had notched up sales of over three million copies worldwide, but Nadia was still trapped in the Yemen. Many people were wanting to know what had happened after the first book was completed.

I still wake up in the middle of the night, bathed in sweat and shaking with fear, having dreamed that, having gone back to Yemen to see Nadia ten years later, I am trapped once more.

It all seems so real. I can feel the smallness of the room we're sitting in and the prying eyes of the villagers as they watch us. Some of them are silently suspicious and hostile. Others are shouting abuse at me for all the trouble I've caused them, all the shame that I've brought down upon them in the eyes of the world.

In my dreams they know how much we hate them and that we will do anything to escape. They know that we see them as our enemies and they are afraid of us, though they are the ones with all the power. They are able to dictate what will happen in our lives whilst we seem able to do no more than embarrass and temporarily inconvenience them.

But I'm no longer completely powerless as I was in the eight years that I lived there, either in my nightmares or in my waking life. I know now that I can fight and that I can win some battles. But no matter what I do, the Yemeni men are still in control. They are still able to threaten and abuse us and make us fear for our lives and the lives of our children. They can still do whatever they want to Nadia and there seems to be nothing we can do to stop them.

They can sell our children, or make them work, or send them away.

Sometimes in the dreams I have taken my car with me – that treasured symbol of the freedom which I hold so dear – and I've managed to get Nadia and the children into it, along with some of my friends and relatives from England. It's a small car and we're all crushed in like sardines. We are so close our thunderous heartbeats are as one as we struggle to start the engine and make the machine move forward. The men are getting closer and I know that the car will be no protection unless I can get it to move quickly. They will overwhelm us, tip the car over and shake us out, like emptying coins from a child's money-box. We have to get away but there are too many of us for the little car and we're weighing it down.

It would have been hard to describe Zana's dreams in the third person without the readers wondering how on earth I, as a biographer, would know about them. There would be an immediate assumption that I was making them up for dramatic impact and a doubt would arise as to how much more of the book could be believed. As it is, we were able to use the dream sequence as the opening words, giving us a chance to set the scene for people who hadn't read *Sold*, without too much laborious repetition for those readers who had already read it and were keen to find out what happened next.

The joy of proliferating

The speed with which you can gather the information for a ghosted book means that you can produce far more publishable material in the course of a year than if you were researching each book in order to write them under your own name. For anyone who has a fertile curiosity and who loves the actual process of writing, this provides the greatest joy of ghosting.

In the 1990s for instance, I was commissioned to write the autobiography of a Chinese billionaire living in Kuala Lumpur. It was at a time when the Far Eastern economies were particularly strong and the business community in the West was worried that they were going to be losing their position of world dominance. Men like my client were sitting on top of the world and to get even an hour of his time as a journalist or potential biographer would have almost impossible. As his ghostwriter, however, I was given all the access I needed to learn about his life in a world I had previously known virtually nothing about. I had, when working as a travel writer, been to many of the places that he had operated in, but I still had no idea how he would have lived as a child. I had seen the simple little villages amongst the towering dark rubber plantations and paddy fields, but I couldn't have any notion of how it felt to go from being a small barefoot boy tapping rubber from the tops of trees in the early hours of the morning to being one of the richest men in the world. To find out how it felt to live under Japanese occupation, and to endure the racial tensions in Malaysia during the years following the Second World War would have taken me endless hours of research and interviewing in a country where I had no contacts and only understood English.

But as a ghostwriter I could ask the man the questions directly and compress the months of research into days. It was the Great Gatsby theory in practice again (see pp. 3–4), dipping my toe into a fascinating world about which I had previously known nothing, observing and learning and then returning home to create a memoir for a man who had lived through momentous times – whose father had left China as a coolie, with nothing more than a sleeping mat rolled up under his arm, but who had escaped from his past and now had control of tens of billions of dollars.

It was a great story that I would never have had the time or money to research for myself from scratch. But because I could turn it round within a reasonably short space of time, I was able to make the project financially viable as well as a fascinating experience.

Because publishers are also willing to pay higher advances for books by well-known authors, since they can see how they will market the book once it is written, and because of the speed with which the books can be turned around, ghosting makes it quite possible for an unknown writer to make a good full-time living as an author. Any unknown who has tried to earn a living from books written under their own name will know just what an uphill struggle that is. The exact statistics are hard to pin down, but what is quite certain is that most professional authors make very little money indeed from their writings, usually not enough to be a sole source of income and certainly not enough to support a family with any degree of comfort. Ghosting can make the difference between being able to earn a living from writing, and not being able to.

Experience and contacts

The great 'Catch 22' of an industry like publishing is that you need to have good contacts in order to get your material hauled to safety from the slush pile and read, and you need to have a track record of success in order to win people's trust. But how do you achieve that if you have no contacts or experience in the first place? To gain a reputation you need to be published, but you need to have a reputation in order to convince a publisher to commission you.

Most people who flirt with the idea of being a writer come up against this stumbling block very early on in their careers and never move any further. But ghosting can give you a way around the problem. It provides broad writing experience and helps you to build contacts in the publishing industry to whom you can then sell other projects of your own at a later date. To begin with, you can demonstrate that you are reliable by turning in material of a publishable quality on time and working with the editor in a professional manner. You will also be able to show that you can structure a book, holding the reader's attention all the way through. You will be able to demonstrate that you can grasp subjects and stories easily and write in a convincing style, no matter what voice the author has.

Writers often complain about feeling like outsiders in the publishing business, seeing agents, editors and booksellers as working on the inside of the industry. It's easy to become paranoid when you spend the majority of your working life alone with a computer screen. By becoming a professional ghost you are one step closer to being a publishing insider, without actually having to get a nine-to-five job and commute to an office somewhere. If you do the job well you will come to be seen as a useful resource rather than a necessary nuisance; as a professional craftsman rather than a temperamental artist. (I dare say some publishers will deny that they ever see writers as a nuisance, but I would suspect they are lying.)

More information about the skills needed by a ghost can be found in Chapter 11, *The Necessary Skills*, on pp. 137–45.

Asking impertinent questions of interesting people

Of all the advantages that ghosting offers, one of the greatest must be the opportunities that you get to meet people of interest. It's a licence to ask the sort of impertinent questions to which you truly want to know the answers, and to be allowed inside some of the most extraordinary stories.

Ghosting a book for someone is like being paid to be educated by the best teachers in the world. Imagine, for instance, being asked to ghost *The Origin of the Species* for Darwin, or *The Decline and Fall of the Roman Empire* for Gibbon; being paid to learn everything that is in their heads and then turning their thoughts, words and notes into book form. Could there be a better form of education?

It also allows you to ask whatever questions you want without fear of giving offence or being rebuffed. How often have you met someone at a party and really wanted to ask them how much they earn? Who they're sleeping with? How they got to be where they are today? Why on earth they married whoever they did marry? When you're a ghost you can ask all these questions and your subject will be obliged to answer, even if the information they give you won't make it into the final manuscript. Journalists can ask the same questions, of course, but will often be rebuffed due to the atmosphere of distrust that exists between much of the media and people in the public eye. The ghostwriter, on the other hand, is there specifically to understand the truth about the subject and the story. It is a position with privileges more akin to the family lawyer than the investigative journalist.

Why become a ghostwriter:

Ghosting gives you access to stories you might otherwise never come across.

It allows you to enter worlds you might otherwise never be invited into, and to ask impertinent questions of interesting people.

It allows for a faster turnaround of projects and improves your chances of earning a good living.

It provides valuable writing experience.

It helps you to build up contacts within the business.

It increases your chances of receiving decent advances.

It means that someone else can do the promotional work while you get on with the next book.

Writing in the first person singular can help to make stories both dramatic and affecting.

2

Why Not to Become a Ghostwriter

Alert readers may already have noticed that this chapter is not nearly as long as the preceding one, and from that gather that my views are going to be weighted more towards the positive than the negative. Having sung the praises of my chosen profession so fulsomely, however, I think it may be only fair to temper the praise with just a peppering of possible negatives. However much I enjoy it, I must concede that ghosting will not be for everyone. If you are temperamentally unsuited for it, then the whole process is likely to become a nightmare.

Too many opinions of your own

Many people take up writing because they have powerful opinions that they wish to convey to the world. Such people will find ghosting hard, since it is largely about conveying other people's views – whether you agree with them or not. If you prefer voicing your own opinions to listening to other people's, you might find the ghosting process uncomfortable since you will constantly be wanting to interrupt them and take the floor for yourself, both during the interview phase and on the page.

Your views may be highly considered and the result of a fine education, but still completely unsuitable for the job in hand. It is no good writing a book in the voice of a 15-year-old girl and saying things that a 40-year-old man (if that is what you are) might say: it is her opinions that the reader has paid to hear, not yours. If you are ghosting for an East End gangster it is quite pointless banging on about the need for law and order and why they should bring back hanging, unless these are views that the gangster happens to share having undergone some sort of transformation.

17

Too shy

Others take to a life of writing because they relish the solitary aspect of the work and do not enjoy having to interact with others. While ghosting still allows you to spend the majority of your time alone with your computer screen, you do also need to be able to spend a concentrated amount of time with your subjects, during which you're going to need to be in charge of the conversation most of the time. You will not be doing much talking, but you will be doing a lot of guiding. If you are painfully shy or find it hard to get others into a relaxed and confident state, then ghosting might not be for you.

Too preoccupied

If you are in the middle of writing projects of your own, and your thoughts are heavily dominated by the plot of your next novel or the details of some non-fiction book you are undertaking, you might not be in a position to take on a ghosting project which requires you to clear your mind and see the world through the eyes of someone else.

Many professional writers have taken on ghosting projects now and again, when they have been between projects of their own and have stumbled across someone with a story or an expertise who is looking for writing help. That is very different from actually setting out to look for ghosting work as a main source of income. In order to make a success of ghosting you have to be able to give your whole mind to finding and writing the projects.

The ego problem

If you feel that your ego will not be able to stand the strain of seeing your work coming out under someone else's name, then ghosting definitely isn't the job for you. In my experience I don't find that many people – including my own family and friends – notice even when a book does come out with my name on it, so I can't see that it makes much difference.

There is a generally held belief, however, that one of the main reasons people write books is for the pleasure of seeing their names in print. While I don't deny that it is always nice to be credited for work you have done, I cannot see why people who create books, films and television programmes feel quite such an urge to thrust their names in front of their eventual customers.

If I was a car designer and I had created a completely new design for the Ford motor company, I would not be affronted to see Henry Ford's name, rather than my own, emblazoned on the front and back of the car. No one expects a politician to thank their speechwriters after receiving a standing ovation for their stirring words. Yet most people involved in book or script writing, acting, directing and allied trades feel they have to have their name on the product. It does not necessarily have to be so.

Once you have accepted that most of the pleasure in being a writer comes from simply being able to do the job and being paid for it, the urge to see your name splashed across the cover should recede. If you don't think it will, then it might be best to steer clear of ghosting. It's true that sometimes the ghost is credited on the cover, or thanked in the acknowledgements, which is very gratifying; but this can never be relied upon.

The ethical problem

There are those who have doubts about the ethics of someone pretending to write a book when it is, in fact, the work of someone else. If you have any such problems you probably won't find ghosting a pleasurable experience. The chances are you won't have opened this book anyway.

Personally, I don't have any difficulty with the ethics of the practice. I have more admiration for an author who credits the ghost openly in the acknowledgements, even though the cover of the book may give the impression that it is his or her own work, than I do for someone who actually pretends that they sat down and wrote the whole thing themselves. In my experience, however, very few subjects actually want to lie about the authorship situation. In fact, they're often horrified at the thought that their fans might think they're putting on airs and graces and pretending they can do something they can't.

More often it is the publishers or the subject's lawyers and managers who insist that the ghost remains entirely invisible. As long as everyone knows where they stand from the beginning, I don't think the ghost is ever in a position to complain. They know what they are being asked to do from the outset and agree to the terms.

As to whether the reading public is being cheated when a ghostwriter is used, I don't believe that the majority of them care who wrote the book as long as it's interesting, entertaining and easy to read. Those who give the matter any thought would probably work out that a busy actress, business tycoon or gangster is unlikely to have taken the time off work in order to write 80,000 words of glittering prose.

When we listen to a president or prime minister giving a speech, we're all aware that the actual words have been created for him by someone else, but we don't expect him to give the speechwriter credit at the end – and we assume that if he's speaking the words, then he also believes in them. We're quite happy to think of it as 'his' speech, regardless of who actually strung the sentences together.

Reasons why you might not enjoy ghosting:

You may have a preference for voicing opinions, rather than listening to them.

You may feel uncomfortable about asking too many questions of your subject.

You may be too preoccupied with your own thoughts, or possess too powerful an ego.

You may feel uncomfortable with the ethical dimension of the job.

3

Why Do People Use Ghosts?

In order to know how to sell your services as a ghost, you need first to understand why people might be interested in using those services. Any marketing person will tell you that you must understand the needs of your potential customer before you can sell them anything. Creating a product and then trying to find someone who wants to buy it is always going to be harder than finding out what the customer really needs – and then offering to provide it.

They can't write

It may be that your subject simply believes they can't write the book or article themselves.

I tend to believe that virtually anyone who can talk coherently can write; but then I have also been told by innumerable people that anyone can be taught to sing and I know very well that there is no way in the world my brain will ever get my mouth to produce a sound that is anywhere close to being musical or in tune. So I'm willing to accept that I may be wrong about the writing ability thing and that there may be people out there who truly can't get their thoughts down on paper in the way they would want, any more than they could paint a satisfactory self-portrait of themselves in oils or pass an audition for the Royal Ballet Company.

These people make excellent clients for ghosts. They have no illusions about their own abilities and frequently have no pretensions to being literary. They're nearly always a delight to work for, happy to leave the writing process to the professional, just as I am happy to leave the maintenance of my car to a trained mechanic and willing, if reluctantly, to leave the singing to Tom Jones or Robbie Williams.

It's not that these would-be authors are illiterate in any way. The majority of them can write to a good standard when it comes to the needs of their own lives, whether it is for writing letters, reports or even articles. Writing a whole book, however, can be a daunting prospect for anyone, however literate or educated they may be, if they have never done it before. They might be happy writing a 5000- or 10,000-word report or brochure, but it is a big jump from there to holding readers' attention for 80,000 or 100,000 words. I can drive a car, but I wouldn't fancy my chances on a mountain rally or a Formula One track.

They are short of time

Writing a book is going to take at least a couple of months out of your life, even if you're the most experienced author in the world and you know your story or subject inside out. That is a daunting prospect for anyone who has a full schedule. How many senior businessmen, for instance, could afford to take a two-month sabbatical in order to produce a book on management theories?

Talking it through with a professional writer is going to take a few hours or a few days, depending on the depth of the subject and whether some of the material will be coming from other sources. Even the busiest person can envisage being able to spend that much time on a book project.

Most people who have it in them to write interesting books, but who aren't professional writers, are very busy people. They have television series to film, businesses to run, interviews to give, people to train, and private lives which they would like to keep intact. If a ghost can convince them that they will be saved all the time and effort of doing the writing, while still being able to say everything they want to say, they will usually jump at the chance.

In many cases I find that subjects have already had a go at writing their own books by the time they get to me, and may even have managed to get down a couple of chapters, but then have been interrupted by some more pressing matter. The prospect of going back to the word processor and trying to get back into the thoughts they had before they were interrupted is then just too much for them. In other cases they will have poured everything out in a garbled stream of consciousness and have no idea how to structure it in a way that will make it readable. Most often, though, they have produced a few hundred words and the prospect of doing another 80,000 or so is simply too daunting.

Most publishers want books from busy people: no one wants a memoir from a leading lady who is no longer in demand, or a big business man who is sitting at home watching the garden grow. It is almost inevitable, therefore, that they will be short of time. Even if they do undertake to write the book themselves, there is a strong chance that they will get bogged down before the deadline for delivery has arrived. The publication date will be set, the cover designed, the booksellers alerted and both they and the publishers will be desperate for anyone who can save the situation and get the project back on the rails.

English is not their first language

Britain is only a small corner of the English-speaking world, and there are people with stories in every country on Earth. Even if you don't speak a word of another language you can still find people in other countries who can use your help. As well as the obvious places like America and Australia, where English, with only small variations, is the first language, there are also countries dotted all over the world where it is the second language. In those places even well-educated people know that their linguistic skills may not be up to writing books in a language that isn't their own. I have ghosted for clients in the Far East, the Middle East and Africa, all of whom speak English quite well enough to be able to tell their stories clearly and movingly but realise that they cannot write books with the same degree of eloquence. For the ghost, this offers wonderful opportunities to experience different cultures and see inside the heads of people who think entirely differently about many things.

They can't see the wood for the trees

It is often hardest to write about the things you know the most about. If you're writing an autobiography, for instance, your memory is stuffed to bursting with details and trivia about everything from your childhood to the present day. All the people you've met, and all the things you've learned, are jostling to be heard. It can sometimes be impossible to see which will be of interest to someone who doesn't know you personally and which will be too detailed.

A ghost can bring a sense of perspective to the project, seeing the story from the reader's point of view rather than the author's. If someone is writing a book for themselves they might spend a great deal of time and energy describing a childhood holiday they had with a mad aunt, when the aunt actually doesn't appear in the story again and is of limited interest to the readers, who want to move on more swiftly to the author's adult life and achievements.

Someone who knows too much about a subject might also be tempted to use a sort of shorthand that will exclude the more general reader. If, for instance, a high-technology guru wants to write a book to help general senior managers understand how technology can be harnessed to maximum effect in their businesses, he or she might not understand how limited those readers are in their existing understanding of the subject. If the author immediately starts spouting technical jargon and refers in passing to concepts that the reader has never heard of, without explaining them in layman's terms, they are going to lose the reader's attention very quickly and the book will have failed to fulfil its brief.

Often, would-be authors ask journalists they already know to ghost their books for them. An actress, for instance, might ask a showbusiness writer she has met; or a jockey might ask a racing correspondent from one of the national papers. The potential problem there – although at first it may seem like an advantage – is that both the subject and the ghost will know the same things. The jockey will be able to refer to a particularly famous race and the writer will immediately know what he is talking about – and may assume that the reader does as well. Any reader, therefore, who is not similarly steeped in the folklore of racing (which will include most general readers) will feel left out and unable to follow what is being talked about.

A ghost who has only a lay knowledge of the subject will be able to keep asking the same questions as the lay reader, and will therefore open up the potential readership of the book to a much wider audience.

They need a ghost as 'therapist'

I have often been told by subjects that by the end of the research process, they feel as if they have been in therapy. Although some are nervous about baring their souls to a stranger at the beginning of the operation, they often warm to the process of talking about themselves (particularly in the case of autobiographers), or about their skills (in the case of 'how to' books). The very fact that they have embarked on the creation of a book suggests that they have a strong ego and will therefore welcome a chance to talk about their favourite subject to someone who is non-judgemental, truly wants to listen and can be trusted not to betray their confidence at any stage of the process.

For most people it is a far more pleasant experience to sit down and talk about themselves for a few hours, than to sit at a keyboard for months on end trying to achieve the same result.

They need your contacts and experience

In some cases a ghostwriter is the subject's first contact in the publishing industry. An established celebrity will probably already have a literary agent who knows which publishers to approach, and who can advise on how to get the best deal. Someone who comes from outside the publishing industry and has simply got a great story to tell will be in a different position and may have no idea where to start.

When Zana Muhsen first approached me she had been a virtual slave in the Yemen since she was 15. She certainly didn't have any idea of how the publishing industry works, or who she should approach in order to get a book into the shops. She asked at her local library and they gave her my telephone number. I was then able to help her prepare a synopsis for *Sold* and find a literary agent who would be willing to represent us. The agent then took over as the guardian of her interests, but I, as the ghost, had been her first point of contact with the industry.

With Donya Al-Nahi, author of *Heroine of the Desert*, I performed a similar function. She tracked me down, having read *Sold*, and asked if I would be interested in her story about snatching back children in international 'tugs of love'. We went through the same process and found an agent; that agent, however, was not able to place the book with a publisher. I still felt confident that it was a potential bestseller and so took it to a couple of publishers I knew, both of whom made offers within a few days. Most publishers today won't even look at any unsolicited material that hasn't come through a known literary agency, but if a ghost has publishing contacts of their own, they can sometimes short-circuit the system and get the subject a first foothold on the ladder.

More than one author

Sometimes you come across people who want to write a book in conjunction with someone else, as well as using a ghost. I had that experience with Lizzie Anders and Katie Hayes, two young women who had survived one of the bloodiest hijacks in aviation history. They had been travelling together on Ethiopian Airways Flight ET961, when hijackers took over and the plane crashed. It had been the most terrifying experience and both of them had learned an enormous amount about themselves and about the meaning of life. They wanted to write a book together, but they also wanted to get back to their travels once they had recovered their health, so I was hired to piece the story together for them. We decided to do it as alternate chapters, one by Katie and then one by Lizzie.

To make things even trickier we had to communicate by letter during the writing process because they were constantly on the move around the globe. The book, *Hijack*, worked well in the end, giving an insight into what it is like to endure the nightmare that every one of us dreads happening at some time in our lives. One of the main reasons it worked, however, was the extraordinarily good relationship that the two women had. Not many people would have been able to pull off such a feat.

Why would anyone want to write a book at all?

In most cases there is an element of vanity involved in writing a book. Authors always believe that they have something of interest to say; they want people to listen to them, and a book is a good medium for both. This is not always true, of course. Zana Muhsen's sole objective was to draw international attention to the fact that her sister was still imprisoned as a virtual slave in the mountains of Yemen. The fact that she had no other self-interest in telling the story was, I believe, what made her such an attractive character to the reader, and resulted in the enormous sales.

Publication of a book will often help the authors in other areas. If they are celebrities it will help them to reach wider audiences, or to 'set the record straight' if they feel that they have been misrepresented in the media or that the public has misunderstood them. Those authors who are in business can use books as marketing tools. A management consultant who has written a book on the subject will find it a useful method of impressing potential clients, and the same principles apply in virtually every profession from cooking and gardening to the practices of law or accountancy.

For many, however, the production of a book will simply be a money-making venture in itself. An out-of-work actor may be able to boost their chances of employment with a memoir about their past affairs with other, more famous actors, and they will certainly be able to make some money from the publishing and serialisation deals to tide them over their sticky patch. Using a ghostwriter means they will be paid more quickly than if they struggle with writing the manuscript themselves and, if it is well written and well presented, they will probably be paid a higher sum.

Why publishers use ghosts

Although there are some publishers who remain convinced that all ghostwritten books are somehow inferior – and I doubt if they will ever be convinced otherwise – publishers often like to use ghosts because they know they will be able to rely on them as professionals. They want to know that the book will arrive on time in a publishable form, conforming as nearly as possible to the synopsis or the brief.

If the author of the book is not a professional writer, there is a strong possibility that any manuscript they turn in will need a great deal of time-consuming editing. The publishers would much prefer to have that work done by a ghost at the beginning of the operation than try to explain to a temperamental star that their prose really isn't up to a publishable standard. (The American publisher who tried telling this to Joan Collins ended up being thoroughly and expensively trounced in the courts and the international media.) Editors are extremely overworked in most modern publishing houses and do not have time to do complete re-writes of manuscripts under the pressure of looming deadlines. A ghostwriter, on the other hand, has plenty of time because that is what they do for a living. They do not have to attend budgeting meetings or sales meetings, or editorial planning meetings, or any of the other daily meetings that editors are forced to attend in the course of their jobs.

The ghost can also act as a go-between for the publisher and the author. Authors are often busy people and hard to get hold of; sometimes they are temperamental. The publishers consequently rely on the ghosts to make the process of publication as smooth as possible.

The ghost often remains the subject's best friend in the publishing business even after the writing stage is over, or at least inactive. During the long months when the agent is trying to sell the project and the phone doesn't ring, the ghost will be assuring them that this is perfectly normal and doesn't mean they will never find a publisher. When the publisher wants to change the title or favours a cover in the subject's least favourite colour, the ghost can again be there to assure them that it will all be okay on the night. Then, when the book comes out and the subject can't find it on the front table in any of their local book shops, the ghost will have to explain the sad realities of the business to them and try to dissuade them from ringing the publisher and ranting and raving. It may be, however, that by that stage the agent has taken over as the subject's best friend. But in those situations, whom will the subject then come to when they want to moan about the agent? You guessed it, the ghost.

Why agents use ghosts

Agents will usually call upon the services of ghostwriters when they have a project which they're sure they can sell to publishers in theory, but which they're having trouble getting started. If they've managed to persuade a particularly hot actress or footballer to confess all in an autobiography, they want to be able to go to publishers quickly with an irresistible package. They do not want to have to wait until the star has the time to write something themselves, even if they have the ability to do so.

If the agent has approached the star with the idea of the book in the first place, they may have overcome an initial reluctance to take on the daunting task of writing by offering to find a suitable ghost for them. The agent knows that the ghost will understand the needs of the marketplace and will be willing and able to quickly produce a professional synopsis and sample material that will convince publishers to start a bidding war.

Writing for celebrities

Publishers and agents are always trying to get celebrities to put their names to books. In a market where it is so hard to bring your product to the attention of the customer, a celebrity name is a powerful marketing tool. However, the fact that the publisher wants them to write a book doesn't mean that the celebrity will be able to – and ghosts will often be called in to bridge the gap.

To start with, there are the biographies and autobiographies of anyone who has managed to get themselves into the public eye. Many celebrities, of course, have become famous because they've led interesting lives or have achieved great things. Such books are easy to write because there is so much to be said.

At the same time there are a great many people who have become famous simply because they appear on television, and have never actually done anything else of any interest or distinction. Their only selling point is the familiarity of their names and faces to a wide section of the public. Trying to write an interesting book about someone when all they're doing is listing shows they've been in and people they've met who are even more famous than themselves, is a very uphill struggle, and the resulting tomes are usually pretty bad and only of interest to die-hard fans.

If the celebrity is going to use the book to make a startling confession (e.g. they had an affair with a prime minister, were bi-sexual, abused by their parents, raped by a famous boyfriend or suffered from drug addiction or alcoholism), that book may only make financial sense because a newspaper will buy serialisation rights just to get hold of that one revelation, but it may still be rather a boring job for the ghost if there isn't anything else of interest to fill the rest of the pages.

To make a celebrity autobiography interesting a ghost really needs to be looking for stories that have a number of different levels. Gillian Taylforth is a good example of the perfect celebrity subject. Not only is she a well-known name through her television work, she is also of interest to the newspapers because of her private life. Apart from being one of the nicest and most genuine people in the business, she also had the courage to take on the might of Rupert Murdoch's News International Corporation, and had lost a major law case in the glare of the spotlight. The story therefore was of a normal London girl from a strong family background suddenly finding herself catapulted to fame and having to deal both with a voracious media with no protection from her employers, and with finding her way around the legal jungle where ruthless big-time lawyers stalk their prey. It was not just a story about funny things that might or might not have happened on the set of *EastEnders*, but also a portrait of an amazingly courageous woman who is enormously popular with everyone she comes across. Just being an actor or pop singer does not make someone an interesting person.

Having said that, ghosts who are offered celebrity work will seldom turn it down, even if the author is not the most fascinating of subjects. It's always fun to hang around film studios and backstage at pop concerts. As you get to know the star you usually fall under the spell of their charm and manage to find other facets of their life that make the project sufficiently interesting to hold your attention and satisfy the publishers.

Getting on with the celebrities themselves is often the easiest part of the operation. It is their 'people' who tend to make the ghost's life a misery. Managers and personal assistants protect their employer's time while lawyers put up every possible barrier to simplicity they can think of, from insisting on enormously long contracts to haggling about every last penny of the Croatian second serialisation rights. It is important at the beginning of the project to find one person in the star's entourage who is reasonable and keen to see the book happen, so that they can be your champion inside the camp if things get difficult. That role can sometimes be filled by the literary agent (see chapter 7), but they can find themselves as frustrated as the ghost by the star's 'people' whose job seems to be solely to make life more complicated.

The ghost will also be under pressure from the publishers to dig up something controversial that they can use to sell serial rights and to generate publicity at the time of publication. If the author can be persuaded to confess to one of the heinous crimes that the tabloid media are so keen on reporting, the publishers know they are more likely to be able to recoup some of the money they will have paid out to the star. While the publishers are trying to get the ghost to find out more, the star's public relations and legal advisers will be trying to get them to tell as little as possible. So sometimes, ghosts can find themselves stuck in the middle. In such situations all you can do is explain to the star what it is that everyone wants, and then tell them to make the final decision about what goes in and what stays out.

As well as autobiographies, stars do sometimes put their names to other types of publishing project, such as dieting or joke books, or publications to do with programmes they have presented or appeared in. In those cases the ghost will probably not even meet the celebrity. The publisher will be the one who works with the ghost to decide on what goes into the book and the star will merely lend his or her name to the cover and possibly do some promotional work at the time of publication.

Writing for experts

One of the reasons that experts frequently need the services of ghosts is that they don't realise just how much more they know about their subject than anyone else. If a professor of genetic engineering wants to write a book for others in the industry, or to be used as a teaching manual for students, they may be better able to write it themselves than if it is a book for the general public. While the general reading public may have a great interest in genetic engineering, it understands almost nothing about the subject. It needs to have some very basic concepts spelled out before it can begin to understand the finer points that the professor might be wanting to put across.

With the same level of knowledge as the average potential reader, the ghost will know what questions to ask, and will be able to predict when arguments and explanations have become too complex and need to be simplified or illustrated.

If the professor has given a complicated explanation on how cloning works, the ghost could then come back with ideas on how to relate that to things that we all understand. Is there an analogy to be found in industrial mass production, or in cookery or some other more mundane activity that everyone can relate to?

Similarly, a financial director wanting to write a popular book on money management needs to remember that many of the readers will be experts in sales or marketing or human resources and not finance, and will need to have things explained in terms that are more familiar and every-day.

A ghost can be an enormous help in turning an expert into a great teacher, in being the one who translates the knowledge that is in the expert's head into a language that others with none of that knowledge can understand.

When a ghost shows the first draft of a manuscript to an expert author, that expert may worry that it is too simplistic, thinking that their peers might see it and underestimate the depth of their knowledge. The ghost must keep stressing that the book is being aimed at a specific target market, and if necessary get the publisher and agent to reinforce that message.

Hopefully, the process of writing the book will force the author to think more carefully about how to communicate on their subject to new audiences.

Would-be authors may use ghosts because:

They believe they don't have the ability to write.

They don't have the time to do it.

They are too close to the subject matter and need a wider perspective.

They want someone to talk to.

They want a guide in the publishing jungle.

Publishers want to know there is a professional doing the writing, making it closer to a risk-free venture.

Agents want someone who can make a pet project into a reality.

4

How to Get Started

Some writers stumble into ghosting by accident. Someone with a story to tell meets a writer socially, hears what they do for a living and suggests that they pool their resources and write a book together. If the writer likes the person and has nothing else on at the time, they may well agree. Many of those who find themselves in this situation will never ghost again once the project is over; not because it has been an unpleasant experience for them (although it may have been), but because they have other work they want to do and don't think of ghosting as being an occupation they want to actively pursue. If another ghosting project falls into their laps they will do it, but if it doesn't they will get on with other things.

If you actively want to work as a ghost, then you can't afford to wait until the perfect project drops from the heavens. It might happen tomorrow, of course, but it is more likely that it will never happen at all. You're going to have to go out hunting for work, and there are a number of different places you could start searching.

Approaching your heroes

The first step could be to approach people you think you would like to ghost for and offer them your services. That might mean your favourite celebrities, whom you could write to care of their agents or television companies; or sportspeople, whom you could contact through their clubs.

On the other hand you might want to approach less well-known people you have read about in the papers, and who have stories that could be developed into books. It's usually possible to find some way of getting a letter or e-mail to them. They might have been the victims of a particularly dramatic kidnapping, or they might have been working in the Third World building orphanages; perhaps they have saved an animal species from extinction, cycled round the world or been diving for lost treasure. In any newspaper there are always stories of people who are not household names, but who have tremendous stories to tell: try seeking them out and asking if they have considered writing a book about their adventures.

The bigger the name, the harder it will be to convince people that they should use your services – especially if you are inexperienced. But even successful people are usually pleased to hear from writers who are enthusiastic about the same things as they are.

The more experienced you can demonstrate yourself to be in any area of writing, the more comfortable people will be using your services. Often, though, it comes down to simply approaching the right person at the right time – i.e. luck.

The man or woman next door

A more practical first step, however, might be to approach people whom you come across in everyday life and who have an expertise that you think would be popular with a wider audience. There is no reason why you can't be making approaches to both types of subject at the same time.

If you've been on a course, for instance, find out if the trainer has thought of turning their message into book form. Would a garage mechanic who's good at explaining why your car isn't working be able to supply the material for a book on car maintenance? What about your doctor doing a book on healthcare for a specialist sector of the market? How about an alternative healer who believes in the power of rune stones, or a clairvoyant who claims they can see into the future? The options are endless.

I once decided I needed to go on a public speaking course, as I was being asked to give speeches about ghostwriting and to make presentations about various books I was writing. I rang several well-known training consultancies. It was quite early in the morning and at one of them, the Kingstree Group, the telephone staff weren't yet in and the managing director, Lee

Bowman, picked up the phone. Used to dealing with big corporations more often than individuals, he asked what I did for a living and I explained. He suggested that I come on the course for free and then ghost a book on *High Impact Business Presentations* in his name for a share of the royalties. I was happy to accept, took the course, found a publisher and the book was in the shops about a year later.

Make sure you tell everyone you meet what you do for a living. You will be amazed how many people are thinking of writing a book but know they need help – or know of someone else who is thinking of writing a book. Most leads will come to dead ends, but every so often someone you meet at a dinner party or down the pub will actually produce a story or an expertise that really will work as a book.

I was once being interviewed about ghostwriting by a journalist from the *Daily Telegraph*. We were sitting having coffee in an airport hotel lounge. When we got up to go through to the dining room for lunch, a man stood up from a meeting at a nearby table and asked for my phone number, having overheard what we were talking about. It turned out he wanted to hire the services of a ghost but hadn't known where to find one. So don't be shy about talking about your profession because you never know who might be listening.

Business subjects

Think of all the companies there are in the world, and all the money they spend on trying to get their messages across to potential customers and to the world in general. Every one of them is a potential author of a ghosted book.

Any expert who has access to a captive marketplace, like training companies or public speakers, has a ready-made market for books. If a few hundred people turn up to a seminar, paying several hundred or even several thousand pounds for the privilege, they are going to think nothing of shelling out a few more pounds for a book by the person they have come to listen to. Just as people will buy souvenir programmes when they go to the theatre, an inspiring speaker will make the audience want to know more about their subject. Approach anyone you know who has an audience of any kind that could be reached through a book and offer to help them write one. ✻

There are companies who might want to produce books by their chief executives for distribution to employees as well as the outside world, and there are public relations departments who would relish the idea of getting their clients' messages to wider audiences.

Make sure in your approach that you point out all the potential marketing benefits of a book. That way, even if it is going to be little more than an ego-trip for the chief executive, at least they will be able to justify the costs internally. Make sure they also understand that you are offering to undertake virtually all the work, so they don't feel daunted by the apparent size of the project.

Family histories

This is an excellent area for the beginner to practise their craft and build up some experience. These are stories that won't necessarily find homes with traditional publishers or get into the bookshops, but are still worthwhile tales to tell. I often receive calls from people who have an elderly relative who would like to set down their life in book form before it is too late, wanting to leave a record behind for future generations. They have no expectation of creating a bestseller or of seeing their faces on the shelves of WH Smith, but they still want to get their memories into print, or at least down on paper or on disk so that they can be printed later if required.

Everybody has a book in them, or so the saying goes, and the older they are the more they have to say. The problem is that there just isn't enough time in the world for everyone to have their story read by more than a handful of interested parties. Grandma's memoirs might only ever be of interest to half a dozen descendants; not enough to make them a viable proposition for a professional publisher, but that doesn't mean she can't commission someone to write them for her.

In this situation a ghostwriter is performing much the same function as a portrait painter, using words instead of canvas and paint. All the skills that are required to produce the big bestseller are needed in just the same way if the book is to be readable. The potential rewards may not be so great (although some people are willing to pay a great deal to get a good writer on their side), but the work is easier to come by. People who have been in the military, for instance, are always good sources of material, having had adventures in battle and having travelled the world.

Often people who have overcome illnesses or addictions or difficult childhoods want to commit their experiences to paper in order to inspire others. A very brave woman whose son had died in mysterious circumstances once approached me. She wanted to write about her experiences so that others who had lost their children in similar ways could see that they weren't alone. She realised that the chances of persuading a publisher to buy the book were slight, so she had it printed up herself and sold copies through relevant charities and church groups with an aim to helping other bereaved parents.

Starting with articles

Writing a book is a major undertaking for anyone, whether they are the author or the ghostwriter. In order to break the ice you might start by suggesting to a potential subject that you first ghost articles in their name. If they are business people, for instance, you might write something for their trade papers; if they are local characters then create something for them to publish in the local paper. If they are a celebrity you might suggest that you could produce a regular column for them, which could be sold to a national magazine or newspaper. An actress might do a cooking or health column; a socialite might talk about the parties she's been to that week; a hairdresser might write about hairstyles that have been in the news, or hair care problems.

They might suggest the subject matter for the articles themselves, or you might need to think the ideas up and then ask for their opinions. Once you've won their trust they might be happy to let you create the articles in their names without even bothering to check the copy personally. I have even come across celebrities who haven't bothered to read their own autobiographies, having complete faith in their ghosts to represent them accurately.

Once you've built a rapport with the subject you can think

about ways in which you could develop the articles into a book. You will also by then have a wealth of material that you can show to publishers, to give them an idea of what the tone of the book will be, and to convince them that your subject is a known expert on whatever the content might be.

Use your existing contacts

If you're already a writer in another field, approach your existing contacts with suggestions for ghosting projects. A showbusiness journalist, for instance, has access to actors and singers. A sports writer can approach sportspeople they've interviewed in the past. People will nearly always prefer to work with a ghost they already know and trust and feel they have a rapport with, than with a stranger.

Bear in mind, however, that you may need to aim this book at people who know less about the subject that you and the author do. If you are a sports writer, for instance, specialising in football, you will be used to writing for people who read the sports pages every day and know who you are talking about without you having to go into too much background detail. If you then write the autobiography of a World Cup player who appeals to young girls as a sex symbol as well as to football fans, you'll need to explain some of the finer points of football in more detail than you are used to doing.

Announcing your ghosting intentions to the publishing industry

At the same time as approaching potential authors, you should also be letting the publishing world know that you're available for ghosting work.

Most people who are looking for a ghost will start by asking someone else in the business. Zana Muhsen went to her local library; others might ask in their local bookshop or approach a literary agent, a publisher or another writer. You need to ensure that as many of these people as possible know how to find you when they need you.

The difficulty is that there are very few people who use ghost-writers on a regular basis. Most authors only use them once, and even prolific ones will only use them once a year. Most publishers and agents will need the services of a ghost at some stage, but who can predict when that stage will be? The only way to be sure they will approach you when the need arises is to get your details onto their desks at precisely the right moment.

That means that, statistically speaking, you're probably going to have to approach hundreds of people before you strike lucky and land on the right desk at the right moment.

Write letters

Write letters and e-mails to all the literary agents and publishers whose names and addresses you can find. (The lists in A&C Black's *Writers' and Artists' Yearbook* would be the best source.) Tell them what your experience is, what sort of work you are looking for and how they can contact you. Some will respond to you politely, saying they'll keep your name on their files. Most will ignore you, but one or two may give you a chance to prove yourself – and that's all you need to get started.

The first two ghosting projects that I got after the management guru had introduced me to the concept, resulted from speculative letters to publishers arriving just as they were pondering what to do with authors who weren't able to deliver the manuscripts that had been commissioned; one was a showbusiness memoir, the other a company history.

Advertise

This is where you have to be more careful, since advertising can become very expensive, particularly when you're just starting out and when you're in a business where the results are so unpredictable. I have been advertising in the publishing trade press on both sides of the Atlantic for over a decade and sometimes I will go for months between enquiries directly generated from the ads. But the enquiries that have come have been enough for me to build a career, most of them leading on to other projects after the initial one has been completed.

The danger is that you will take an expensive series of ads and get no response at all for a year. It's just like buying lottery tickets; the week you stop advertising (or stop buying the lottery tickets) may be the week that someone picks up that magazine looking for a ghostwriter (or your numbers come out of the barrel). It takes nerves of steel to keep advertising during the quiet periods. It is probably not a good idea to start advertising until you know that you can keep it going for a long time.

If you're looking to write for the private market, family histories or business books, then advertising might be a more predictable method of attracting business. A small ad in a magazine for the over-50s, or a military magazine, or even a national newspaper, is likely to generate more enquiries than one in a publishing trade paper. What proportion of those enquiries will actually end up bearing fruit is anyone's guess. In this situation, however, it is probably possible to gauge the effectiveness of a particular medium pretty quickly, so that you can get out of it as soon as it is obviously not paying dividends.

On the one hand I would not recommend a commitment to advertising unless you can afford to lose the money. On the other, I have to say that no one ever achieved anything in life without taking a risk. Only you can make the call on that one!

Build a website

The Internet is a godsend for writers. It is there for the storage, rearrangement and communication of information (the same description could fit the professional writer). The costs of setting up your own site are minute, compared to advertising in magazines and newspapers. Once you have actually created the site – and you can spend as much or as little as you choose on that – you can just leave it there, paying a nominal amount each year to keep your domain name. There are plenty of professionals around now who specialise in helping people to build sites and their charges are very reasonable.

The Net's greatest advantage for British writers is that the American market is far more comfortable using it than are Europeans, and they have far fewer worries about dealing with a ghost in Britain than they would have if they were relying on the old-fashioned telephone and airmail services. Ten years ago when I was dealing with American clients I was forever having to send out bulky manuscripts at enormous cost, and waiting days for responses. Telephone calls were so expensive as to be out of the question for all but the most profitable projects. Now it is as easy to deal with someone on the other side of the world as it is to deal with someone on the other side of town. In a couple of cases I've managed to write whole books with clients via the Internet, without even having met them and having only occasionally spoken to them on the phone. Within a year of setting up my website (www.andrewcrofts.com) it had paid for itself a hundredfold and most of that work had come from America.

Once your site is up and running, you can take your time thinking of ways to bring it to the attention of potential customers through advertising or direct mail. All the time more and more people will be discovering it for themselves, and more and more people will be recommending it to others and creating links with their own sites (as long as you have made your site interesting enough).

How you design it will depend on how you're planning to market yourself, but you need to make it clear that you are a ghostwriter or co-author, or whatever you like to call it, and that you are looking for people to work with.

DIY PR

Get yourself interviewed, quoted and written about in the media wherever possible. I have found that whenever a journalist has written a story about me or quoted me in a general article about ghostwriting, potential clients have made contact as a result. Editorial coverage is free advertising (as long as they're saying nice things about you), and reaches a far wider audience. It's also much more believable. I can say in an ad that I am a successful ghostwriter, but anyone who reads it is going to know that is just my own opinion. If a journalist says it in a newspaper or on the radio, the readers or audience will have no reason to doubt it.

Approach editors and suggest that you write an article on ghosting or on your latest project if your subject doesn't mind. If you have the nerve, suggest that they do a feature on you. Start with your local paper and work upwards. The worst they can do is say no.

Things to do to get yourself started:

Contact everyone famous you would like to ghost for.

Scour the papers for good stories which could be developed into books and approach the participants.

Approach everyone you know personally who might have a book in them.

Approach businesses that might benefit from publishing a book.

Offer your services to people wanting to write books for private distribution.

Start by ghosting articles.

Develop your existing contacts and experience.

Write to everyone in the publishing industry, telling them what you do.

Consider advertising to target markets.

Start planning a website.

Launch your own public relations campaign.

5

Who Pays the Ghost?

This is a touchy subject. When you're juggling with people's life stories and fragile egos it's hard to bring up the sordid topic of coin without sounding heartless and mercenary. But if you're going to be a professional ghost you have to be sure you can generate enough money to support yourself and your dependents. There are no set rules here, which makes it harder in one way, but leaves greater room for flexibility when there are good stories on offer but little money to finance the writing of them at the start.

There are a number of different ways in which you can organise how you are paid for your work, and I will look at each of them in turn.

Hedge your bets

The safest way to work is to hedge your bets – by mixing your portfolio, and doing some work for fixed fees and some speculative work for a percentage of the possible profits.

Like any punter, or any City fund manager for that matter, sometimes you'll back the right horses and sometimes you'll back the ones that don't even make it out of their stalls; but by spreading the bet, you are minimising the risk of losing everything when you have a run of bad luck.

I was recently approached by a young man wanting to write his autobiography. He suggested that we write it as a partnership, dividing up any money that the book eventually made. This is an arrangement I have often found to work well, but in order for it to be successful I have to be confident that we can find a publisher who is willing to pay a large enough advance to support me during the writing process, having only seen a synopsis.

Although I liked the young man enormously and thought his story was very moving, I was not sure that we would be able to convince a publisher without showing them the whole manuscript. I was not sufficiently confident of success to be willing to write the whole book speculatively.

Regretfully, I told him of my misgivings but he insisted that he wanted to go ahead anyway and was willing to pay me for my trouble. I quoted him a reasonable fee, which I was confident he could afford. We wrote the book and I introduced him to an agent who sold the book to a publisher within four days, for a sum nearly ten times the amount I had been paid – and that was just the advance! Had he not had the courage of his convictions and been willing to put his money where his mouth was, the book would never have been written and I would never have known what I had missed. I could tell many more stories of projects for which I agreed to take a percentage and ended up earning less than the minimum wage for my labours, and others for which taking a fee was the right thing to do. I could also point to those for which a share of the royalties has come out to far more than any fee I would ever have had the nerve to charge.

Every time you make a decision on how you will charge for a book, you're placing a bet. Sometimes you will win big-time, and sometimes you won't, but you still need to cover your losses.

Books paid for by the author

How the ghost gets paid will depend largely on how speculative the project is, and on the wishes of the author. It might be that the author is sufficiently confident of the book's success, as in the case of the young man above, to suggest paying the ghost a fee. Sometimes they may even not want to approach publishers: I have had clients who simply wanted to record their lives for posterity and to put the resulting manuscript in a bank vault to await future generations. More often they just want to get the material recorded in some way. Then, if a publisher shows an interest later on, so much the better.

In all these situations the ghost obviously has to charge a fee because there probably won't be any royalties. How much that fee will be depends on what the author can afford, what they are willing to pay and what the ghost is willing to do the job for. In other words, it's open for negotiation.

As the ghost, you must decide how much money you would need for the time the project is likely to take. Make it crystal clear that you are giving no guarantees that the book will ever find a publisher or that the author will ever recover their outlay to you. They must understand how hard it is to sell a book and that, no matter how well you write it for them, they still may never see it in print unless they are willing to self-publish it.

If they are still keen to go ahead after that, and you find the story interesting enough to want to spend time on it, then go ahead.

I generally suggest that the author pay half of the agreed fee at the beginning of the project and the other half once they have accepted the manuscript. Sometimes they might prefer to break it down into a series of monthly payments, or payments at different stages of the operation. As long as both of you are comfortable with the arrangement it doesn't matter how it is structured.

It may be that you can hedge your bets yet again and agree to a reduced fee plus a small percentage of whatever the book might earn. That way the subject will know that you are as keen to make the book good as he or she is, and you will be able to dream every now and again about how you will spend your percentage when the book becomes a bestseller and the millions start to roll in. Personally, I like to keep the sums as simple as possible.

How much should you charge?

This is an almost impossible question to answer. However, when you have decided to take a fee and are asked to name a price, there are some basic equations that you can work out in order to give yourself an idea of what to charge.

Before you go into the negotiation process you need to have asked yourself certain questions:

- How much do I need to earn each month to live?
- How long is this project likely to take?

- Will I enjoy the work or is there a boredom factor involved?
- How much can they afford?
- How much would they expect to pay?
- How long is the manuscript going to be, roughly?

Some of these answers will have to be guesswork, but you can still have an idea. So, let's pick a figure out of the air and assume that the minimum you can live on is £2000 a month. You think that the book will take three months to write, so the least you can possibly ask for is £6000, unless you're willing to take a loss in order to get the job. If the author is very short of money (in which case it might be better to take a different option and split the money), then £6000 is probably all you can charge and you just have to decide whether you want to do it for that much or whether you want a share of the royalties as well. If they're very wealthy and you know they're used to paying reasonable amounts for services, then you can adjust the figure to one that seems more realistic. A billionaire who is going to be flying you around the world at his beck and call for three months is not going to expect to have to pay the same as a retired colonel down the road who wants to write a book about his war experiences. (You may still decide to do the colonel's book as well as the billionaire's, because you like him, he lives close by and doesn't make unreasonable demands.)

The minimum figure isn't truly realistic, because at the beginning of your career you will not be earning in every month of the year. This project may have to provide you with enough money to live for six months, until you get the next paying job, meaning that £12,000 would be more realistic. If you are more established and have a lot of overheads you may have to set your minimum rate much higher. This will mean that some people won't be able to afford you, but you should be able to compensate for that loss by winning more of the higher-paying jobs.

At the same time you may be willing to drop below your minimum figure and take a loss on some jobs, particularly at the beginning, just in order to win them and start to build up experience and a portfolio of published work.

So every job is different and only you can come up with the right price for each one.

Payment by length

Although the concept of selling words 'by the yard' is slightly disconcerting, you do have to take the prospective duration of a project into account. An 80,000-word manuscript is likely to take almost twice as long as a 40,000-word one. It looks obvious when you actually spell it out, but it is all too easy to give a quote for writing a book without taking this into account. A fee that might be realistic for a two-month project might be wholly inadequate for a four-month one.

Make sure you have a rough idea of how many words you can produce in an averagely productive week, as well as working out a minimum figure for the amount you need to live on per week.

Fees from publishers

If a publisher has a project that they want to publish, but realise that they will need to use a ghost, they may suggest paying a straight fee for the work. There are a number of advantages to accepting this sort of arrangement, provided that the fee is realistic.

To begin with, there is nothing speculative about the work because the publisher has already committed to publishing. It will also give you a chance to impress them with the professionalism of your approach and the dexterity of your writing. If you do a good job they will be extremely grateful to you for getting them out of a hole and will be much more open to any suggestions you might later bring to them for other projects. It will also give you another book to put on your CV, which is particularly valuable when you are just starting out.

In these situations there probably won't be much room for negotiation. The publishers will suggest a price that they are willing to pay and, although you may be able to edge them up a little, the given sum is probably more or less all that is available. As you get more experienced you may be in a stronger position to haggle, but the likelihood is that there will always be other writers more desperate than you who will be happy to do the work, however low the price. When you are just starting out, you should accept any book that is offered by a publisher, even if the money is low, simply in order to build up a track record. (When you look back ten years later you will remember first the book and the experience of writing it, and you will be less concerned about how much you were paid.) Even for the experienced writer the relief of knowing you have a publisher on board from the beginning is worth dropping your price for, particularly if it is an interesting project.

Sometimes, however, publishers will take liberties and suggest a price that simply isn't economic. If the work is likely to take you three months and they're only offering enough for you to survive on for one month, you will need to point this out to them and politely decline, unless you can afford to work for free for two months in order to do a project that interests you, and can make the difference up on other books.

Dividing the spoils

Frequently, an author is not in a position to pay a ghostwriter the sort of money they would need to cover their time; and usually, no publisher has been found at the time the author approaches the ghost. These are the projects where you have to take a leap of faith and agree to work speculatively and to share in pre-arranged percentages whatever money the book does or doesn't earn. In some cases (worst scenario), that will mean writing the whole book 'on spec', but more often it will mean creating a synopsis that can be used as a selling document to raise an advance from a publisher. I will talk in considerable detail about how to ghost effective synopses later in the book.

Virtually every ghosting project is high-risk. Anyone who has tried selling books to publishers will know that rejection is the norm, and that even when you get accepted the chances are the money will be considerably less than you would have earned if you had been sweeping the streets instead of sitting at your keyboard. Every so often, however, you will have a book that will take off and compensate you for all the ones that didn't.

Almost all ghosts will have to do some speculative work if they want to keep enough projects on the go to make a steady living. I would suspect that over the last ten years my success rate with speculative synopses has been one in three: for every story that I managed to find a publisher for, two didn't find homes. And that is a pretty good hit rate.

If one in ten of those books that found a publisher becomes a bestseller, that is enough to make ghosting a highly profitable proposition. The problem is, however, you will never be able to predict in advance which will be the one to reap the big rewards. Sometimes the money will come from a big serialisation deal with a newspaper, sometimes it will come from translation rights to other countries. Occasionally it will come from film or television rights and sometimes it will simply come from sales in Britain.

I work on the theory that if the project that has been brought to me interests me, and if I think there's a chance it will be published,; I'm willing to do some speculative work on it. I will suggest to the author that we split whatever the book earns 50/50, which includes advances, royalties and foreign rights sales, serialisation fees and payments for film and television rights.

If the author is a celebrity and it's obvious that the book will make a large amount of money, the ghost might have to accept a lower percentage – or a percentage that will become lower once he or she has received a pre-agreed amount. For example, the proceeds might be split 50/50 until the ghost has received £50,000, at which stage his or her share might then drop off to 40%, and then drop again at £100,000. However, I always prefer to make the financial side of the deal as simple to understand as possible, which is why I like 50/50: the last thing I want to do is to have to pay accountants and lawyers to work out complicated divisions later on.

It would be unwise to write an entire book 'on spec' unless *some* money has been forthcoming, either from a publisher or from the author, but there are cases where even this risk is worth taking. With fiction it is nearly always necessary to write the whole book before any publisher will make an offer, making it a highly risky business (see pp. 131–6). Go into it with your eyes open, knowing that every project you take on in this manner is closer to buying a lottery ticket than earning a living.

The best thing about owning a percentage of a book is the excitement of dreaming about the millions it might make for you, and then the wonderful realisation every so often that you have a real winner on your hands. There is no buzz like the one when an agent or publisher calls to tell you they have just done a six-figure deal for serialisation or sold translation rights in another country for a property that you own a piece of.

Expenses

Again, there are no golden rules. If you are being paid a very low fee, then you need to ensure that there aren't going to be any expenses that will mean the project ends up costing you money rather than making it. If you're working on a percentage then you will probably have to find your own expenses from the start, just as the subject will have to find theirs. Assuming that you are already set up with a computer and e-mail, the worst costs are likely to be travel. Make sure you know what these are likely to be before you start and make it clear who is going to be footing any bills that might occur.

I tend not to charge expenses unless there are going to be major items like air tickets and hotel bills. If the expenses are going to be high, make sure you have covered them in some way, unless you are very confident of a profitable outcome from whatever the project might be.

I suspect that if I added up all the money I have spent on travelling to see people for projects that never earned a penny I would feel too ill to continue writing this book, so I won't do it. But if I hadn't invested that money at the beginning, I wouldn't have found the gems that have ended up providing me with my living.

The rules for getting paid:

Hedge your bets with a mixture of differently constructed deals.

Have some guaranteed money coming in to keep you alive and some pipe dreams to keep you awake.

Work out the least money you need to survive and make that your minimum rate.

If publishers approach you direct, take the work (unless the fee is an absolute insult), so that you can go back to them with other projects later.

Make sure you won't be paying unreasonable expenses.

6

Contracts – Do You Need Them?

I hate dealing with contracts and lawyers, which is why I usually work through literary agents and let them handle all the details (see pp. 61–7). I tend to believe that if you trust someone enough, you don't need to tie them up with contracts – but I know that in some cases that is unrealistic. Sometimes you need to have something in writing that you can refer back to, should anyone forget what the original deal was; and you do need to be covered against some of the things that might go wrong.

The contracts you will have with publishers are fairly standard. What you have to think of first is how to word the agreement between yourself and the author.

The confidentiality issue

When a would-be author first contacts me, they're often understandably nervous about giving away too much. The contact has probably been made over the phone or by e-mail and they have no way of knowing if they can trust me or not. If they're famous they may be worried that I'll sell their secrets to the tabloids (most celebrities have been betrayed too often to give their trust to strangers easily), and if they aren't famous they may be worried that I'll steal their story and write it myself. (I try to explain to the latter that it will be hard enough selling the idea under their own name, let alone mine, but they can't always be convinced.)

The problem is that in order to give a reasoned opinion on the merits of their story and whether I can help them, I need them to tell me what it is about. One way of winning their confidence is to offer to sign a confidentiality agreement, so they know that whatever they say at this stage will go no further. It makes no difference to you as the ghost what you sign regarding confidentiality, since you have to be discreet about clients if you want to build a reputation for being completely reliable. If you start dashing off to the newspapers with every titbit of gossip that comes your way you'll soon find the calls drying up.

Once you've agreed to do the book, the author may still want some sort of insurance that you won't use anything you find out in the course of the research in any way they wouldn't want you to, and you may need to put their mind at rest by signing something on that too. The caller may already have drawn up a contract themselves, but if they haven't, you can suggest sending them something along the following lines. (This is a real example, but would need to be adapted for different circumstances. The main objective is to make the subject feel comfortable talking about personal, dangerous or controversial matters.)

Dear Mr Bloggs,

This letter is to confirm the terms and conditions pursuant to which you are prepared to disclose details of your story to me.

1. This undertaking shall be binding upon me and all my employees, agents or professional advisers (together 'Relevant Persons').
2. This undertaking extends to all information of whatever nature in whatever form relating to the book obtained from any source, including without limitation, information received from the owner.
3. I shall treat all confidential information as being strictly private and confidential, and shall take all steps necessary to prevent it from being disclosed or made public to any third party by any relevant person or coming by any means into the possession of any third party.
4. I shall use the confidential information for the purpose of writing an outline for submission to the publishers and, on conclusion of a publishing agreement for the writing of the book, I shall not use any part of the confidential information for any other purpose whatsoever.
5. I shall not use or disclose or permit the disclosure by

any person of the confidential information for the benefit of any third party or in such a way as to procure that
I may at any time obtain commercial advantage over
the Owner without prior permission of the Owner.
6. Neither I nor the relevant persons shall by any means
copy or part with possession of the whole or any part
of the confidential information without prior permission of the Owner.
7. The confidential information and its circulation shall be
restricted to circulation and disclosure to individuals
whose identity shall have been approved by the Owner
prior to disclosure.
8. I shall keep all materials containing confidential information in a safe and secure place.

Signed ...
Dated ...

In most cases I find that just the offer to provide such a document is enough to put their minds at rest; rarely do you actually
have to go to the trouble of signing anything. Once the relationship has got underway, a bond of trust will form – because without it, no agreement would have been reached anyway, and the
subject won't arise again.

The libel problem

Libel is a very real danger for anyone writing a book. When
you're ghosting for someone else it becomes particularly tricky.
If you're writing a book under your own name you can make
sure you don't publish anything that you haven't checked to be
true and non-libellous. When you're ghosting, however, you're
often taking the author's word for something. If they promise,
with their hands on their hearts, that they had an affair with the
Queen of Ruritania, or saw the Queen's husband murdering the
butler's gay brother, you are going to want to put that in the
book, and there is little you can do to ascertain its truthfulness.
What you don't want is for the Ruritanian royal solicitors to
then sue you for libel.

You do need, therefore, to have something in the contract to say that anything the subject tells you that turns out to be libellous is not your fault. Similarly, the author needs to be covered in case you slip in some extra fact of your own which turns out to be untrue.

In most cases I have felt that I trusted the word of the person I was working with, having spent some time getting to know them. There have been times, however, when I have realised during the process of listening to the story, that they are people who see the truth through a sort of prism of self-interest, or have simply become confused between fantasy and fact. In those cases I have always taken extra care to check every fact – but even so, there are times when stories slip through that may differ from other people's versions of events. In one particularly memorable case a whole print run of a book had to be withdrawn and pulped because the author had claimed an affair with someone in the public eye who was furious at the very suggestion and immediately set lawyers onto the case.

A simple paragraph in a letter of agreement or contract will iron this sort of potential problem out (see pp. 58–60). In the case described above, I was very relieved that an agent had insisted on inserting words that let me off the hook. Even though there was still a subsequent loss of earnings because the publishers lost confidence in the author as a result and didn't republish the book, at least I wasn't liable to be dragged through the courts.

The division of labour

In terms of the division of labour, basically you just need to agree that the author will provide you with as much information as possible and that you will write the book to the best of your abilities. There really isn't much else that either of you can guarantee the other, apart from the method of payment and the libel and confidentiality issues. It is amazing, however, how many contractual pages a highly paid lawyer can drag those simple agreements out to if given his or her head.

It is important that the subject realise they have to provide you with enough material to work from, either in the spoken or written form. Sometimes they think that if they spend an hour or two briefing you then that will be enough for you to spin out an entire book. You have to make it clear to them that unless you are given enough material, you'll have to start imagining the rest – which may make the final product very different from how they had envisaged it, since it will be written in the voice of the ghost rather than the voice of the subject. If they aren't going to give you the information themselves, then they must be able to point you to other people who can fill in the gaps.

They must also be prepared to read the manuscript through and explain what changes they want to make, unless they're willing to trust the ghost completely and sign off on the project unseen. It is surprising how many are willing to do that. It does speed the publishing process up, but makes it awkward if there is a factual error, which they would have picked up by reading it through.

The whole point of the arrangement is that the ghost will do by far the lion's share of the work, but the subject must be aware of the possible consequences if they avoid all responsibility for the final text.

By-lines

If you have agreed to have your name appear on the book in a certain way then you can also have that written into the contract at this stage, although bear in mind that whatever you agree with the author won't necessarily be agreed by the publisher.

Approval

To ensure that the subject feels completely confident about talking freely, it's a good idea to reassure them in writing that nothing will be shown to anyone else, not even the agent or publisher, until they have okayed it. This also means that you are never put in the embarrassing position of having handed a manuscript in and then having to come back to the publisher and ask to take some bits out that the author doesn't like.

A simple letter of agreement

If the author wants to prepare a major contract, then by all means allow them to do so, as long as they realise that they will be paying the lawyers' fees. If an agent is involved at this stage, they may well have a standard collaboration agreement for authors and ghosts, which will cover all the necessary points. When I'm asked to prepare a contract, in the interests of simplicity I like to send something along the lines of the following letter to the author once we have met and decided to go ahead.

Dear ....,

This letter is to clarify both our understandings of how we will work together on your life story.

1. You will give me all the information you want included in the book.
2. I will turn the material into a typescript.
3. I will not show that manuscript to anyone until you have okayed it. I will make whatever changes you request.
4. I will not discuss or write about anything we talk about in the course of preparing the book, other than in the manuscript which you get to see.
5. You agree to indemnify me against any claims for libel or damages which arise from information you have given me.
6. I agree to indemnify you against any such claims which arise from information I supply.
7. We will divide equally all monies that are earned by the manuscript.

Signed ...
Dated ...

A simple contract

If you're wanting something a little more formal, the following might be a useful template to work from. This contract was drawn up without an agent and includes, in point 6, a commitment from me to look for one. If you're not confident that you could provide a useful service in this area, it would be better not to promise it. The chances are, however, that the ghost will know more about selling a manuscript to the industry than the subject.

Memorandum of Agreement made this 1st day of January 2004 between Joe Bloggs and Andrew Crofts acting for themselves and their respective heirs, executors and assigns: Whereas Joe Bloggs has invited Andrew Crofts to collaborate with him on a memoir/family history.

IT IS HEREBY AGREED BETWEEN THE TWO PARTIES AS FOLLOWS:

1. In consideration of the duties undertaken by Andrew Crofts he shall receive 50% of all income due from the book until such time as he has received £100,000, from which time he will receive 40% of all income due from the book, including, but not limited to, book, film, television and serial rights.
2. Joe Bloggs fully indemnifies Andrew Crofts against all claims for libel or breach of copyright that may be brought against the Work by any party relating to material supplied by him and Andrew Crofts fully indemnifies Joe Bloggs against all claims for libel or breach of copyright that may be brought against the Work by any party relating to material supplied by him.
3. The parties hereby agree that, to the degree that it is in their power to ensure, all editions shall state that the book is by Joe Bloggs and Andrew Crofts.
4. All copyrights, renewals and extensions shall be jointly owned by Joe Bloggs and Andrew Crofts.
5. Andrew Crofts will be primarily responsible for writing the book based on material supplied by Joe Bloggs, and agrees to show the resulting manuscript to no one until Joe Bloggs has given permission. He will make whatever changes Joe Bloggs requires. Joe Bloggs will be responsible for the provision of any photographic material for use in the book that the publishers may require which is

within his power to supply.

6. Andrew Crofts will suggest an agent to act on both their behalfs who will deduct his/her previously agreed commission before distributing money to Joe Bloggs and Andrew Crofts in the proportions laid out above. Andrew Crofts will undertake an introduction to that agent and ensure that he/she is supplied with all the material necessary for selling the book to a publisher.

IN WITNESS WHEREOF THE HANDS OF THE SAID PARTIES

If you are at all doubtful about your situation, and you don't have an agent to advise you, you can always ask a solicitor to draw something up for you. In my experience, however, lawyers tend to make things over-complicated, and the chances are that even if things do go wrong, you're still not going to want to waste a lot of time and money suing the author. All the contract needs to do is make the author feel relaxed, comfortable and safe, and put on record whatever has been agreed so that you can refer back to it at a later date should there be any disagreements or misunderstandings.

Some helpful legal steps:

Draw up a confidentiality agreement if it makes the author feel more comfortable about talking.

Get the author to indemnify you against any libel claims.

Lay out what has been agreed about the division of labour and division of monies.

Agree to let the author see everything you write before you submit it to anyone else.

Do anything necessary to engender an atmosphere of trust and confidence between the two of you.

Avoid lawyers if at all possible.

7

Do You Need a Literary Agent?

There are a number of reasons why you may need a literary agent.

To start with, most publishers now refuse to read anything that hasn't been submitted through a recognised agency. Some ghosts may be sufficiently well connected to be able to bypass this roadblock at one or two publishers, but they will not be able to get into as many as a good agent can.

Agents also provide a very useful service. They may charge a percentage (usually 10 or 15%) on whatever monies they manage to get for you, but they more than earn it by getting the price higher and negotiating on the rights. They also take away all the hassle of checking contracts, chasing up late payments and everything else that can take up a writer's precious time.

I often find it helpful to have a third person in the relationship with the authors I work for. It means that the authors and I never have to talk about money or contracts or anything else that is likely to be contentious. In the event of a problem or misunderstanding arising we can both talk to the agent, who can then find a solution, leaving our delicate relationship intact.

It is equally helpful to have a fourth person in the relationship with the publisher. If anything goes wrong you want the agent to be the one who falls out with them, not you or your author.

An agent can be a very useful first sounding-board for an idea. If someone approaches you about a book idea and you have one or two agents who will take your calls, you can run it by them very quickly before committing any time to the project on spec. If they completely squash it then you might be well advised to pass on the offer and look for something else. Equally, they might help you to see the best way of approaching the synopsis in order to make it attractive to the marketplace.

It *is* possible to survive without an agent, but since they now control most of the books sold to publishers which would involve the services of a ghost (academic writers being probably the largest exception to this rule), you ignore them at your peril. Having said that, agents are not infallible. They are not always as evangelical about a project as you or your author might be, since it will be only one of dozens that they're trying to sell. They may give up trying before you would. Most agents will send an idea out to a dozen or so publishers and if they all say no, then that will be the end of it. With a number of projects I have found that every publisher in London or New York has said 'no' except for one, and that one has been the last on the list. *Sold*, for instance, was turned down by every publisher in London apart from one, and went on to sell several million copies around the world. In that situation we were lucky enough to have an agent who believed as passionately about the story as my author and I did, and who refused to give up until the end. I have had other books where I have managed to sell the rights myself after the agent has given up trying. Despite this drawback, I would always prefer to have a good agent on-side if possible.

The only way to find an agent is to have at least a strong synopsis prepared (see pp. 68–99), and at best a full manuscript. You then need to write to them asking if they would be interested in seeing it with a view to representing you.

At what stage do you get an agent?

This depends. You may already have an agent for other literary endeavours and be legally obliged to channel all your ghosting work through them, having signed some sort of exclusivity agreement with them. (Try to avoid doing this if you can, but I realise it's hard if you're starting out and can't get a foot in the door any other way.) If the relationship is good that will be fine, but it will mean you are limited in your dealings with other agents who might want to use your services as a ghost for their clients. It is my experience that the more agents who know about your skills, the better.

In some cases the agent will come to you attached to the author. You can then either allow that agent to handle the deal on behalf of both of you, or you can put him or her in touch with your existing agent and let them work out the relationship between them.

I tend to be in favour of there being only one agent involved, handling the whole deal on behalf of both the author and the ghost. I don't want my agent to be haggling about money or by-lines with the author's agent; in that situation, my agent is going to feel it is his or her prime duty to look after my interests rather than those of the book. I would rather we were all focused on the same goal of making the pot as big as possible for everyone. Other ghosts feel much happier always dealing with the same agent, which is fine if it works for them.

It may be that the author will come to you without an agent and so you'll have to go looking for one together. If you already have a contract with one agent, you'll have to go there. But what will happen if they say no, they don't like the idea, or don't think they can sell it? Are you just going to give up, or are you going to endanger your relationship with that agent by going off for a second opinion somewhere else?

I would prefer to circumvent that problem by not being tied to any one agent but taking the author to one I think he or she will get on with and who I think will do a good job with that kind of book. Different agents are good at different things: some are skilled at dealing with big celebrities and fighting for major serialisation deals, while others are good at molly-coddling a newcomer who is unsure of themselves. Some are one-man bands while others are part of huge international organisations. There are some who will never take on a book until they have read it through several times and are completely sure they'll get a sale, while others will do little more than read a one-page syn-opsis before going out into the market and swearing that this is the biggest potential seller since the Bible.

Several publishers have admitted to me that when some agents call and announce who they are, the publishers immedi-ately know that they're going to have to add several noughts to whatever offer they might have been thinking of making for the agent's product. That sort of agent works well for the big block-buster books, but might not be much use for something that is going to attract lower advance offers.

If you're approached by a publisher direct, you'll have no trouble finding an agent to represent you, since they'll know that they don't have to do any selling and that the job is as definite as it is possible to be. The problem there is that the agent might not be able to make any difference to the terms of the offer if the publisher has already made up their mind, and so you'll be paying them a percentage of your fee for nothing. If you are contractually obliged to take such jobs to your existing agent then fair enough; if not, then you might be better off just dealing direct with the publisher.

If you're going to be on a royalty deal, however, then an agent might be able to haggle over terms for you, and will be able to chase up monies at a later stage. In that situation the agency percentage would be worth paying.

If in doubt, get an agent – if only for potential networking opportunities in the future. If you have two to choose from, go for the one you like and trust over the one who makes the biggest promises.

What will they do for you?

A good agent will advise you on how to improve your synopsis or manuscript so that it appeals to publishers. They know which publishers are looking for what sorts of manuscripts and will be able to get fast responses from most of them. They'll be able to save you a lot of wasted time if your idea really isn't likely to work. However, remember that in most cases an agent will only try ten or a dozen different publishers before giving up (although some will become so fond of the idea that they'll keep going until they've tried every publisher possible).

They will negotiate the deal for you. If more than one publisher is interested they'll organise an auction to get you the highest possible price. They'll handle all the paperwork and then chase up the money whenever it's due. It's amazing how big a difference a few small tweaks to a contract can make to the amount of money you receive in the long-term. They might, for instance, insist on retaining the serialisation rights and then sell them separately on your behalf for a figure twice anything the publisher would have got, and the money will come straight to you and your author. Or they might negotiate a separate deal with an American publisher where you might have happily signed away the English-speaking rights for the whole world.

They may also bring you more ghosting work once they're confident of your abilities and grow to like you.

Finally, they will act as an arbitrator between you, the author and the publisher should any problems arise.

Beauty parades

Sometimes literary agents, and indeed publishers, will arrange ghostwriting 'beauty parades' for their clients. If they have on their books a famous footballer or supermodel who has expressed a willingness to write a book provided that a suitable ghost can be found, the agent or publisher will then set up a series of meetings between their illustrious would-be author and possible ghosts. Often they seem to have some difficulty rounding up enough possible suspects to make it seem like they've trawled the market as conscientiously as they might like their client to think.

Some writers take exception to the process, feeling that they're being treated like cattle, but I've always found it a fairly civilised process – nothing like as demeaning as the sort of things the stars themselves probably had to go through in the earlier stages of their careers. Having seen what indignities can be visited upon a young actor or actress auditioning for a role in a toothpaste advertisement, I think asking a ghostwriter to have a friendly lunch with a Hollywood star or a civilised drink in a rock star's hotel suite is hardly arduous. I have always found the subjects to be very polite and respectful, just as anxious to impress their potential ghosts as the ghosts are to impress them.

It always helps if the agent or publisher arranging the meeting already knows your track record and can recommend you personally, but after that it comes down to whether the would-be author likes you enough to want to spend time in your company, telling you their every secret. The rejection, if it comes, is nearly always very gentle. Whenever I have failed to win a beauty parade I have always been told politely that it was because the author wanted someone of the opposite gender, or someone with greater inside knowledge of their subject. I dare say age makes a difference as well, since a 20-year-old pop singer is likely to choose a writer of a similar age over a greybeard who prefers listening to Radio

Two, and a comedian of advancing years is unlikely to want to trust his life story into the hands of someone who's never even seen him perform.

If you are asked to attend a beauty parade, even if you feel that you may not be the best ghost for the job, I think it is always worth accepting. The meetings are usually interesting and it never hurts to have an agent or publisher in your debt.

Sometimes a star's management company will hold a beauty parade of literary agents as well as ghosts. Twice I have had the experience of being rung by three or four different agents on the same day, all of whom have been approached by a star's people and asked to recommend ghosts. In those cases I went to the meetings with the first agents to ring, explaining honestly to the others what had happened.

How do you get an agent?

At the beginning of your career, of course, you'll be happy to find any professional agent who will agree to take on your project. There are a few hundred reputable agents in Britain and a few hundred thousand people trying to get onto their books, so the hardest job will be getting any of them to listen to you at all.

If you have an author and a story but no agent, you will have to undertake a methodical search. The list of potential targets can be found in A & C Black's *Writers' and Artists' Yearbook*. If you have any inside information or introductions that you can call on, then start by approaching them; if you have a blank canvas then you may have to go to almost all of them before you get a result. Begin by sending them the very briefest of letters explaining who you are, who the author is and why you think their story has potential. When an agent responds to that, send them the synopsis you have prepared (see pp. 68–99). They will only respond if they like your idea and if they have the spare capacity to take on more clients. If they remain silent, remember that it isn't personal – it just means they aren't taking on anyone new at the moment because every hour of their day is already filled to bursting.

In some cases getting the attention of a good agent is harder than getting the attention of a good publisher. If you're having difficulty getting any agents' attention but you're still sure that the project has potential, send a similar letter to some publishers. It's just possible that one of them will bite if they are looking for the sort of project you are offering. Once you have a publisher interested you will find it a great deal easier to get an agent on board, since much of the work has already been done for them.

If you don't have to sign any sort of exclusivity deal with any of them, then keep the pressure up by writing speculatively to ask if they have any clients or projects that they need ghosts for. Most of the time you'll be met with a wall of silent rejection, but you only need one success to make the campaign worthwhile. Don't give up until you have tried every possible avenue. Only those who persevere succeed: many people have talent, and many perserverance – but few have both.

Why you need a literary agent:

Many publishers won't look at anything not submitted by an agent.

Agents will make you more money than you can make for yourself.

They will do all the tedious legal and accounting jobs.

They will act as go-betweens for you and the author.

They are a constant potential source of new projects.

They know the business and can advise on every aspect of it.

They will save you a lot of time.

How to get a literary agent:

Keep contacting them with ideas and offers of assistance.

Don't take rejection personally, and perservere.

8

The All-Important Synopsis

This may be the most important chapter in the book, because whether you're going to be a success or a failure as a ghostwriter rests largely on whether or not you can write a synopsis that publishers will buy. You may be able to write the greatest book in the world, but unless you can persuade someone to pay you while you do it you may also starve to death before you get to the last chapter. While an agent can perform a great many of the sales and marketing functions on your behalf, it is down to you to create and package a product that publishers want to buy. There is no way round this.

It's unusual for any publisher to pay an advance for a ghosted book idea without seeing a synopsis and some sample material. The fact that you have written the synopsis in a certain way doesn't mean that you can't adapt and develop the ideas once you're writing the final version. If you compared the synopses that I have given as examples at the end of this chapter with the actual books that eventually came out, you would see significant differences. A synopsis has to be good enough to tempt a publisher – to make them commit to buying your idea so that a competitor doesn't get it – but if you can subsequently think of ways to improve on it, no one will object.

Ideally, the publishers would rather have the completed manuscript, because then they know exactly what they are buying and the risk of anything going wrong is greatly reduced. But they understand that writers have to eat while they're working on a book and so they are usually willing to help out with an advance which they will deduct from any future royalties the book may earn – but which you won't have to repay, even if the book fails to earn enough to cover the advance.

To charge or not to charge?

In many cases you will need to do a synopsis 'on spec', just as you might do a proposal to win a contract in any other industry. In the world of big business it's not unusual for companies to invest thousands of pounds' worth of time in trying to win a piece of business – an investment that they have to write off if a competitor beats them to it. Sometimes you will have to do the same on a ghosting project.

Once you're experienced, you will sometimes be able to charge for writing synopses; but at the beginning it's probably wise to offer to do it for free in order to get some good projects off the ground. The process of creating a synopsis will give you a better chance to discover for yourself whether the author really does have enough material to sustain a full-length book. It also demonstrates to the author, your level of commitment to the project. If you are willing to give up this much of your time on spec, then it is obvious that you believe in them, which helps to cement the relationship at an early stage and to develop an atmosphere of trust. It will also give them a chance to see how you write so that they feel more comfortable when it comes to your preparation of the final manuscript.

It may be, of course, that the opposite happens: and either you discover that there isn't enough meat to make a whole book, or the author discovers that they don't like the way in which you write. In either case, however disappointing it may be, it is better to find out at this stage than after you have put several months' work into producing the finished book.

If an author is going to be paying you a fee for writing the book (see also pp. 45–6), it might be a good idea to suggest that they pay for the synopsis first, subtracting that fee from the eventual cost of writing the whole book. The work you do on the synopsis would have had to be done for the book anyway, so you won't end up out of pocket, and it might be that an author can afford to pay for a synopsis but not for a complete manuscript. If the synopsis then inspires a publisher into coughing up an advance, the author will feel much happier about paying you the higher fee for finishing the job. So, rather than paying you £10,000 for a complete manuscript which might or might not sell, they could pay you £2000 for a synopsis which persuades a publisher to pay the author a £15,000 advance. They will then be able to pay you £8000 to complete the project and still make a £5000 profit.

Each job will be different and how the deal is structured will again depend on what the author can afford and how much you, the ghost, want to take it on. Although it would be nice to be in a position where you could do all synopses for free, you have to be practical. If you reckon on each one taking between one and two weeks to complete, there is a limit to the number of weeks that you can work without reward. It may be, however, that one of these synopses will produce a book contract that is so lucrative it underwrites all the others. This illustrates perfectly both the frustration and the excitement of the ghosting business – you just never know which piece of work is going to produce the jackpot!

The purpose of the synopsis

A synopsis must be a hard-selling document that gives the publisher all the reasons why they should commission the book. It must be something that their sales teams can immediately see how to sell, and that tells their editors the final manuscript won't need too much editorial work on it.

The biggest problem facing any publisher is how to market a book to the public. If you can make it obvious in the synopsis how the book could be brought to the public's attention and why they would be bound to want to buy it, you will be on your way to making the sale. It's always a good idea to name other successful books in the same market sector that you think it could be compared with, and to explain how it differs from any competing titles.

If, through a couple of sample chapters, you can also show the style in which the book is going to be written, you'll put the pubisher's mind at rest even further. A reasonably detailed chapter breakdown (even if you change it later) will convince them that you have thought the book through and will have no difficulty in providing the number of words you are promising. This document must give the publisher confidence that the book will be written to a high standard and delivered on time.

Synopsis layout

The following are suggestions, not rules; they are not written in stone. If you can think of a really eye-catching and unusual way of achieving all the above objectives, then do it. But these ideas might help to point you in the right direction.

Prepare a one-page version of the synopsis first in order to catch their attention quickly. All the people you will be sending this to are busy and will be looking for reasons not to read on: don't give them any. This introduction page should work like the first few paragraphs of a news story in a paper. All the salient facts should be there, but without any detail. Publishers or agents who are not interested at all can see at a glance that it isn't a book for them, and those who are interested can then read on.

The main synopsis can then be a longer document (between 5000 and 10,000 words usually suffices), in order to give a better feel of how the book will be structured and what the author's voice will sound like.

The chapter breakdown can be as short or as detailed as you want, because if the publisher is still reading by that stage they're on the hook and they're looking for reasons to be convinced. Give them as many as possible. It might be that you can combine the synopsis and chapter breakdown by writing a 500- or 1000-word synopsis for each chapter. Each project requires a different treatment and all you're aiming to do is make the document as tempting and easy to read as possible.

A strong title

Finding a suitable title for a book is often much harder than you would think. The best ones, in my experience, offer themselves up at the beginning of the writing process and never change – e.g. *Sold* by Zana Muhsen and *The Kid* by Kevin Lewis. Others end up being the result of endless brainstorming sessions with publishers and seldom carry the same punch. A title needs to convey as much as possible of what the book is about, and also needs to be memorable so that satisfied readers can tell one another about it. Titles are a very subjective business and the author may have strong opinions of their own ... in which case it is better for the ghost to go along with them and let the publisher talk them out of it later if it really is unsuitable.

Sell the author

In your synopsis, include a brief biography of the author and demonstrate how promotable they will be. Explain why they are the world expert on their subject, or why television, radio and newspaper journalists will be falling over themselves to interview them.

Sometimes the authors aren't particularly promotable in themselves, in which case you have to put as much emphasis as possible on the promotability of the material. If it's a book by an elderly professor who isn't going to be willing to talk to the media, you need to stress how important his discoveries are, how blue chip his Curriculum Vitae is and how fascinated the general public are by his subject. If, on the other hand, it is the autobiography of a 20-year-old pop singer, you may need to put the emphasis on their popularity and willingness to perform in the publicity circus at every opportunity rather than on the depth of the material.

Examples

The following are three examples of synopses that sold projects to publishers. The first is a dramatisation of a historical court case which retired journalist, Tom Freeman-Keel, had uncovered and researched and which I then dramatised and turned into a book on his behalf. The publishers that bought it were Carroll and Graf in New York. It quite often happens that people are skilled at either the research or the writing of a book, but find the other a terrible chore. This was the case with Tom and I and so the partnership of researcher and ghost worked well.

The second synopsis is a more straightforward memoir for Donya Al-Nahi, who had achieved some notoriety in the media but was not a household name at the time of writing. People had heard of her exploits but didn't necessarily know much about her. It was therefore the quality of her story that had to be put forward rather than the pulling power of her celebrity. The book was bought by Metro Publishing in London and published as a lead title.

The third synopsis was sold in a large international deal and the eventual book was written with Canadian journalist Helen Slinger and published in Britain by Orion. The author, David McTaggart, was the founder of Greenpeace and had an immaculate pedigree as a campaigner and adventurer. Again he was not a household name, but the organisation that he had built was known all round the world, with many millions of people being sympathetic to the cause. The author himself, sadly, passed away in the early stages of the writing, but the book came out posthumously under the title *Shadow Warrior*.

So, imagine you are a publisher opening your morning mail and try to work out what it was about the following that would catch your attention and make you want to put in an offer.

THE DISAPPEARING DUKE
by Tom Freeman-Keel and Andrew Crofts

This is a true story in which the truth is tantalisingly elusive and the main character steeped in layers of deliberately manufactured mystery.

It is a work of historical detection, following a web of deception and intrigue that continued for over half a century and ended in a headline-grabbing court case. It centres around one of the greatest and most eccentric aristocratic families of the nineteenth century, the Cavendish-Bentincks, at a time when the British aristocracy were at the height of their wealth and power.

It involves fratricide and disputed fortunes, secret underground passages and stately homes, mock burials and clandestine marriages, fraud and bribery, corruption and the financing of a prime minister, perjury and blackmail.

It is also the story of an Establishment cover-up in which witnesses who were likely to expose the truth were cast into asylums or jailed.

The book will appeal to the same readers who enjoyed the

mix of history and mystery in the *The Surgeon of Crowthorne* by Simon Winchester, *La Grande Therese* by Hilary Spurling and the many *Jack the Ripper* books. It will give insights into the bizarre and colourful lives of the rich and aristocratic in the same way as *Georgiana, Duchess of Devonshire* by Amanda Foreman, *Amphibious Thing – the Life of Lord Hervey* by Lucy Moore, *The Warwickshire Scandal* by Elizabeth Hamilton, *Aristocrats* by Stella Tillyard and the many other books which lift the curtain on glamorous and controversial historical figures of the last few centuries, from Oscar Wilde and Bosie Douglas to Fanny Burney and Mrs Jordan.

It will be written in a gripping, narrative style.

The Authors

Tom Freeman-Keel, a retired journalist, has been researching the subject for over ten years. He has compiled a vast collection of evidence in the form of books and photographs, newspaper cuttings and letters, birth, marriage and death certificates, in an attempt to ascertain exactly what did happen in this dramatic story.

Andrew Crofts is an experienced ghostwriter of fiction and non-fiction and has published around 40 books, many of which have become bestsellers.

Synopsis

The book opens in 1848 with an alleged murder inside one of Britain's richest and most powerful families, although no one has ever proved that the allegations were true. It ends with a high-profile court case 50 years later, which made the murder allegations front page headlines and brought into dispute one of the greatest family fortunes in the country.

The central character is the 5th Duke of Portland, a man who was revealed after his death to have led a treble life, each of his identities equally fascinating.

Lord George Bentinck was found dead on 21st September 1848, propped up against a fence near to Welbeck Abbey, the family's magnificent stately home in Nottinghamshire. He was one of the most popular and colourful figures of his time: MP for King's Lynn, Leader of the Protectionist Party, a leading figure on the Turf and Disraeli's major financial benefactor. He was also the favourite of the 4th Duke of Portland's three sons.

In contrast, his elder brother, the heir to the Portland title and his senior by two years, was shy and reserved, avoiding field sports and shunning society.

It was a time of unrest in a country that was dominated by the land-owning families and run from a handful of gentlemen's clubs in London. Robert Peel was introducing his 'peelers' for the protection of the property of the rich, while Britain was entering the disastrous Crimean War and the aristocracy were still nervously watching the aftermath of the French Revolution across the Channel.

The 4th Duke of Portland was fabulously rich and connected by marriage to many of the most influential families in the country. He adored Lord George and scorned his elder son. The family motto was 'Fear of Disgrace', a philosophy that was to influence all their behaviours.

It was alleged at the time that both brothers were in love with the same woman, one 'Annie May' who was the illegitimate daughter of the 5th Earl of Berkeley and therefore a distant relation of theirs. It was whispered that the brothers might have fought, leading to Lord George's death. Newspapers like *The London Times*, which at the time were little more than sycophantic mouthpieces to the Establishment, quoted official sources as claiming that the death was caused by 'a spasm of the heart'.

Behind closed doors, Lord George's death affected political life at the very top, which is another possible reason why the brothers may have fallen out that night. Lord George's loan of £25,000 to Disraeli had allowed the Jewish outsider to purchase a suitable home, Hughenden in Beaconsfield, from which he was launching his campaign for acceptance by the Establishment and eventual rise to power in a Parliament which at the time did not accept Jews. When he inherited the title, the 5th Duke withdrew the family's patronage from Disraeli, although his other younger brother continued to support Queen Victoria's favourite prime minister. The family was integral to the power structure of the day and it's possible that this was what the two brothers quarrelled over on the night of Lord George's death.

The authors will lay out the evidence of what happened on

that night, culminating in the probable murder of Lord George by his brother, suggesting what they believe to be the truth behind the rumours and setting the scene for everything that was to happen subsequently.

The mystery of this death, and the behaviour of the surviving brother who, in due course, inherited the title and all its attendant wealth, would have been successfully suppressed and quickly forgotten about, had it not been for a woman called Mrs Anna Marie Druce, who in 1896, nearly 50 years later, appealed to the Home Secretary on behalf of her son, Sidney George, alleging he was the rightful heir to the Portland and Druce estates, which meant the Dukedom and all its millions. By that time the 5th Duke had been dead for 18 years and a cousin had taken the title.

Her claim opened the whole, very private, family up to public scrutiny. By then the newspapers had lost some of their respect for the Establishment and were willing to print the gossip and rumours that had been circulating in London and Nottinghamshire for half a century. It was a story that would hold the public fascinated for over a decade.

Mrs Druce was an upper middle class widowed woman of limited means who had apparently lived a quiet and respectable life in London until that point. Her son was 21 years old. Her evidence was innocuous and the main platform of her case was that if the coffin of her father-in-law, Thomas Charles Druce was to be exhumed from its vault in Highgate Cemetery it would be found to be empty. She claimed she could prove that he had in fact never existed, but had been a false identity assumed by the 5th Duke of Portland. She claimed that since her father-in-law was the 5th Duke, her son was the 6th Duke not the cousin who had inherited the title. It was an extraordinary claim and the public loved her for making it.

The case, which was one of the longest and most expensive civil court cases in history, became a cause célèbre and the extraordinary double, and later treble, life of the 5th Duke slowly emerged from the mists of time into the spotlight of the printed media. The case lasted for a total of 11 years and destroyed Anna Marie Druce financially and personally. Although the culmination of the publicity was headlines accusing the Duke of murdering his younger brother, the family issued no writs for libel. Their motto, after all, was still 'Fear of Disgrace'.

The case revealed that for many years of his life the 5th Duke of Portland resided at Welbeck Abbey and instigated a massive building programme, creating miles of tunnels big enough for a horse and carriage to travel unseen from the house to the edges of the estate, as well as subterranean apartments, an underground ballroom said to have the finest and most extensive unsupported ceiling of any room in Europe and the second largest riding school in the world, also built beneath the ground. Over 500 masons were employed at Welbeck, joining an estate workforce of over a thousand.

Even on his own estate the Duke lived an extraordinarily secretive life, instructing that no employee should acknowledge him if they saw him. If they met him they were to 'pass him as a tree'. He always carried a large umbrella, wore strange all-covering hats and coats and had his trousers tied tight round the ankles. He ate no butcher's meat, having one chicken killed each day, eating half for lunch and half for supper. He always travelled in a closed carriage, which was conveyed to London by train. The carriage was shrouded in curtains, pulled by six small ponies and driven by young boys. He was never seen at Court and never mingled with society. Even his solicitors were not allowed to interview him. There are no known portraits of this shy man and only one bust. It was claimed that he suffered from a recurrent and disfiguring skin condition. The Establishment was happy to allow him his privacy. Despite the importance of his family and the size of his fortune, he appeared in very few of the biographies written at the time about contemporary figures.

The lack of information available meant that many rumours circulated over the years. There was one amongst London cabbies, which claimed that there was a dead body hidden in a glass coffin on the roof of one of the Duke's London homes, 13 Hyde Park Gardens. Many of the drivers used to arrange to take their fares past the house in order to point it out.

The most startling revelation, however, was that sometimes the Duke would disappear, perhaps for years at a time. Everyone at the time assumed that if he was not at Welbeck he was in London, in a house shielded by specially built 60-foot walls. When he wasn't in London they assumed he was at Welbeck. In fact, he had simply vanished.

At the same time another enormously wealthy man, by the name of Thomas Charles Druce, appeared from nowhere in London. His money, it was later discovered, had been transferred to him by the Duke. The Duke and Mr Druce were, it was proved in the course of the court case instigated by Anna Marie Druce, one and the same person.

Mr Druce bought a huge and prosperous shop called the Baker Street Bazaar, which was reported to provide him with an income of £350,000 a year even then. He proceeded to extend it with a labyrinth of underground passages, one of which was later discovered to lead to the Duke's main London home, Harcourt House. He was also credited with being responsible for the creation of the Alexandra Palace and a number of other mighty undertakings.

By the time Anna Marie Druce brought her case, the 'gutter press', as it was becoming known, was establishing itself, printing stories that the Establishment might prefer to have hushed up. The editors were taking their first tentative steps towards the freedom that we take for granted today, vying with one another for sensational scoops. One paper, *The Weekly Dispatch*, revealed that Thomas Druce had first married a girl called Elizabeth Crickmer when both were 16 years old, and then abandoned her four years later. Elizabeth's parents had not approved of the match since the young Druce, who looked older than his 16 years, would give them no information about his earlier life or substance, and so the young couple had to elope. They apparently lived peacefully together and had two sons, Henry and Charles and a daughter called Frances. Elizabeth had a small fortune of some £15,000 which, it seems from the records, Druce absconded with, leaving her penniless. He then disappeared from the records for 15 years, reappearing in London in 1835 as the wealthy owner of the Baker Street Bazaar.

Further journalistic delving showed that he later lived with a woman called Annie May – who was not the same one that he and his brother were rumoured to have fought over in 1848 – and had Herbert, an illegitimate son by her. In 1851, upon the death of Elizabeth, Druce married Annie May and had another son, Walter who married Anna Marie in 1874. This was Anna Marie's link to the Portland fortune.

The revelation of this earlier marriage was a blow to Anna Marie's case, since it meant that, should she be able to prove that Druce and the Duke were one and the same person, there were at least two other possible heirs to the fortune before her son.

Druce was said to have died in 1864, although the death certificate was not signed by a medical man and various people reported sightings of him after that date, supporting her theory that the burial was a hoax.

That this Mr Druce existed there was no doubt, but when the Court demanded to see a birth certificate, none could be found – no birth certificate and an illegal death certificate. Anna Marie claimed that when her father-in-law became fearful that his double life would be exposed, he announced the death of Thomas Druce, even organising a coffin to be buried in the family vault in Highgate Cemetery containing the supposed remains. She demanded that the coffin should be exhumed and opened to show that it was empty. She said that after her husband's coffin was placed on top of it, Druce's supposed coffin had collapsed; giving this as evidence that there could be nothing inside. She also found a servant who was willing to state that at the time of Druce's death, he was told to bring some lead into the house. Anna Marie suggested that this was in order to make the coffin weigh a realistic amount.

Her petition purported that Thomas Druce had been a pseudonym for the 5th Duke of Portland, and that the Duke had staged the funeral in order to rid himself of his second personality, as it had become burdensome. It was rejected. She tried again and was rejected again. She went on to appeal to the House of Lords, which asked her for a deposit of £10,000 before the case could be heard. The public were becoming increasingly intrigued. The story was front-page news and Mrs Druce borrowed £20 from the *Daily Mail*, a deal reflecting the sort of exclusive offers frequently made to people in the media spotlight today. She claimed she had been offered £60,000 to drop the case and that she had been accosted by two men at Highgate Police Court.

Mrs Druce continued her battle, but the Establishment of the time was still determined to protect its own and ultimately refused permission to open the coffin. Anna Marie Druce was declared insane and placed in a lunatic asylum. Other relatives began to arrive from all over the world, one as far away as Australia, and the case was taken up once again, lasting in the end for a staggering 11 years until the unlimited financial resources of the defence and the might of the Establishment were finally able to crush it. Other witnesses were declared insane and committed to asylums, the tentacles of influence reaching all the way across the Atlantic to New York.

It was also revealed that the Duke, even after he had killed off Mr Druce, was still terrified of exposure and so began to act as if he were mad – presumably so that, should he ever be accused of any crime, he could claim insanity as a defence. Witnesses were found to testify that he took the name Harmer and committed himself to an asylum run by a Dr Forbes Winslow for a year.

The book will provide an insight into how the Establishment of the day worked to protect its own and crush those who attempted to disrupt the existing order, at the same time as telling the gripping tale of deception and detection.

ENDS

There then followed a detailed chapter breakdown, showing how the story would unravel. In the end, the emphasis of the story changed – but the synopsis had still done its work and secured a deal which financed us through the writing period.

I wrote the following synopsis in the first person singular, as if it were written by Donya Al-Nahi herself – although the introductory piece was in the third person, allowing us to 'blow her trumpet' without making her sound conceited. Doing the synopsis in this way had the added benefit of giving the publisher a taste of Donya's voice.

HEROINE OF THE DESERT
by Donya Al-Nahi
with Andrew Crofts

Donya Al-Nahi rescues children for their mothers. Like a modern-day Scarlet Pimpernel, she travels to Middle Eastern countries and snatches back tug-of-love children for desperate women who have given up all hope of being helped by the British or international authorities. By some she is seen as an abductress, but those she helps see her as a modern-day saint and one of the bravest women in Britain.

In 2002, on a trip to Dubai with Sarra Fotheringham, it all went terribly wrong and both women found themselves in jail, facing long sentences. Donya's cover was blown and the media wanted to know more. *The Sunday Times* devoted a whole page to asking who this 'serial kidnapper' was.

Until the final mission, everything was going well. From 12 missions in three years she had successfully returned ten children to their mothers. When she appeared on the *Trisha Show* she received 4000 e-mails from people asking for help or offering support, as well as calls from newspapers and magazines asking to talk to her.

This is Donya's story. As well as being an exciting tale of a series of heart-stopping adventures, it also gives practical insights into what can go wrong when people marry across the culture gap, and tells of Donya's own journey from a troubled childhood and adolescence to becoming a devout Muslim.

Synopsis

It all started with a conversation at a bus stop in Queensway, outside Whiteley's shopping centre. I had all four children with me, including my new baby son, and a woman started talking to me. Like me, and like many other English women in that area of London, she was a converted Muslim. I asked if she had any children and she said, 'Yes, I have a daughter.'

'That's nice,' I said. 'How old is she?'

'She's going to be six soon.'

'Where is she?' I asked.

'She's in Libya.'

'Is she on holiday?'

'No,' she replied and I saw there were tears in her eyes. 'Her father stole her from me six months ago.'

'That's awful!' I was shocked, even though I'd heard of such things happening. 'Do you speak to her?'

'I've had only one phone call from her in all that time.'

I felt sorry for her, but my bus came and I was distracted by the needs of the children. That night, as I was looking at my sleeping daughter, I remembered the woman and it struck me how terrible it would be to have my child taken away from me.

Five months later I bumped into her again in Hyde Park. Like so many of the Muslim women she looked very drab, wearing a long, shapeless brown dress and flat shoes, no make-up and her head swathed in a white scarf. She gave the appearance of someone who'd given up altogether bothering with herself, as if life had defeated her. We got talking again and made a date to meet for coffee.

Over the coming weeks we met quite a few times. Her name was Mary and her daughter was called Leila. She told me how she'd dropped Leila off at her school one morning and then gone back for her at lunchtime, only to be told that her husband had come in soon after the start of the school day to take Leila to a dentist's appointment. By that time the plane for Libya was already in the air.

It was a pattern I grew to recognise. There were always tell-tale signs that the women should have picked up on if they had only known what to look for. The abductions nearly always happen from schools, with tales of doctors' or dentists' appointments, and there is often another man involved; a brother or a cousin or a friend. There have usually been other signs before that. When the fathers start to ask where the child's passport is and begin to show an unusual interest in his or her welfare. If they are out of work and depressed, or begin to criticise England and the English and talk nostalgically about home and about the values of their families, they could also be thinking about returning home with their child. If they start being unusually solicitous and kind to their wives, making them cups of tea when before they have never lifted a finger; that too should sound alarm bells in the wives' minds.

In other cases, once the men begin to think about going home they often start to criticise everything about their wives

82

and the way they are bringing up the child. 'Why are they wearing that short skirt? Why have they got lipstick on?' All the things they used to say they liked about the woman, they now start to criticise.

Usually a small child needs to have a few of their personal possessions with them when they travel, and the mothers sometimes notice that these things have disappeared from the house but still don't put two and two together in time to do anything to stop it. One of the reasons I want to tell my story is to help women in this situation to spot the danger signals in time to avert disaster.

Mary talked about her lost child all the time and I could tell that her heart had been broken. I could see that she was a good woman; that she had been doing all the things she was expected to do in her position; that she'd done nothing to deserve losing her only child. Nobody seemed to be taking any notice of her, or helping her. It didn't seem right to me.

I heard the words, 'I'll go and get her for you,' coming out of my mouth at the same time as she did. I hadn't thought about it all, it just seemed to me that it was the only thing to do in the circumstances. If someone had taken one of my children I wouldn't have been sitting around waiting for the authorities to do something about it; I would have been on a plane. But I could see that Mary was too defeated to be able to do anything by herself and too frightened to be able to think what she would do if she ever reached Libya. With that one sentence I'd committed myself to a whole new way of life.

We started to lay our plans. Mary had just enough money for the two of us to fly out to Libya and stay in a hotel for a few days, but no more. If I was going to be successful in bringing Leila back I was going to have to act quickly and decisively: we didn't have enough money to buy any time. I was fluent in Arabic, having lived for 18 months in Jordan, and Mary had a few words. She had also been to Libya with her husband and knew a bit about the situation we were heading into.

My connection with the Middle East had started when I met my first boyfriend, a Jordanian. I was 15 years old and I left my family for him, going to live with his family in Jordan and becoming a Muslim. I think it started as an act of rebellion against my mother, with whom I had a difficult relationship.

My boyfriend was at university in Watford when we met and he and his family all wanted me to marry him. I loved the Muslim way of life and the people were lovely to me – such hospitality and such wonderful food and smells. I was enchanted. I felt very wanted for the first time in my life. I might easily have been persuaded, but a visit from his brother's wife, who was Welsh, had rung alarm bells in my head. She looked completely defeated and downtrodden and I realised that, if I wasn't careful, this could be me in a few years time. I caught a flight home.

I then went out to Tunisia and met another man who asked me to marry him. I agreed, still on the rebound, I guess, still looking for something to give my life some meaning. But when I turned up for the wedding my future husband had straightened his hair and that shocked me so much it woke me up. I realised I didn't want to marry him. I ran away and hid, but my would-be husband wouldn't return my passport. My Mum had to smuggle me out of the country.

In the year that I'd been in Tunisia, however, I'd become increasingly interested in the Muslim religion that I'd converted to, studying it in college and confirming in my mind that it was the right creed for me.

I was a bit of a wild card in my teens. My next boyfriend was a Saudi multi-millionaire, who moved me into his apartment in Park Lane, took me on holiday to Marbella and bought me a Porsche. Then he told me he was marrying someone else and just wanted me to be his mistress. I was so furious I spent £750,000 on his credit card, without having to sign anything. I ended up being questioned by the American Express fraud squad. Because I hadn't signed anything they couldn't charge me but, not surprisingly, it put an end to the relationship.

Mary travelled with me to Tripoli on her sister's passport, because her sister had her daughter on the same document, which meant we would be able to use it to travel back out with Leila. It also meant we had been able to get a multiple visa, so no one would be suspicious of us travelling around with Leila once we had her.

Tripoli airport was chaotic. It was impossible to tell if there were any systems in place, or whether officials were watching for children being taken out illegally. I wasn't confident that we would be able to get out this way. However much planning we'd done, most of what happened now was going to be down to luck and instinctive reactions. We hired a taxi driver who agreed to take us to the town we needed and to stay with us for about ten pounds a day. When we got there we parked and just sat outside her husband's family home, watching what was going on. Mary had to keep her face hidden in case anyone from the house recognised her.

We stayed there for two days. Each morning a school bus pulled up outside. The driver would honk his horn and Leila would come out of the house and climb in at the corner of the road. It was all I could do to restrain Mary from jumping out of the cab and grabbing her child the first time she saw her.

'Not here,' I told her. 'We need to follow her to school and take her as she gets off the bus.'

That way we'd get a few hours lead before the family realised she'd gone. I'd noticed there were no telephone lines going into the house. That meant someone would have to come physically from the school to inform the family what had happened. There would then be another lapse in time before they got to the police and our details were circulated.

Our return flight was booked for the next day. If we wanted to use that method of escape we had to time everything exactly. We followed the bus to school, about 20 minutes' drive away from the house. My stomach was churning with fear. I felt as if I was about to rob a bank, but I knew that what we were planning was the right thing to do. A mother should never be kept from her child. I glanced at Mary and she looked wild-eyed and close to screaming with the tension as the bus wound its way through the back streets, picking up other children and then heading out into the countryside and on to the next town.

Leila got off the bus as usual. We drew up behind and Mary got out of the car ahead of me. Leila saw her mother and ran over to see her. I was concerned that if things turned nasty the driver might disappear, leaving us with no escape. There was nothing I could do at that stage but trust him. A teacher was standing at the gate counting the children in, so I went over and talked to her, trying to distract her as Mary half dragged her daughter over to the cab, which was waiting with the doors open.

As soon as they reached the car I ran after them and jumped

in, yelling at the driver to go. The taxi sped away from the kerb, leaving the teacher watching, open-mouthed and obviously confused.

Leila's initial excitement at seeing her mother had turned to fear in the midst of the shouting and the slamming of doors and screaming of tyres. She was throwing up as Mary hugged her and sniffed the scent of her hair, as if trying to regain every moment she had lost in the previous year.

As we had a passport under a different name for Leila, I thought it might be worth driving straight to the local airport and getting on the plane to Tripoli, banking on the fact that the police would not be alerting the airport authorities for at least two hours. All the way there it seemed as if every driver on the roads was doing his best to hold us up. I busied myself getting the tickets and passports ready to get straight on the plane. When we arrived we discovered that the flight had been delayed four hours. Could we afford to take the risk of spending four hours in a public place? I decided we couldn't.

Instead, we boarded a boat along the coast to Tripoli and then hired another car, driving across Algeria to Morocco. This was how I would be spending many weeks in the future, driving for hour upon hour, just to put as many borders as possible between the children and the families we'd taken them from. It was sometimes hard on the kids, with the heat of the sun, the dust from the roads and the stops in terrible, flyblown little cafés and shops for refreshments and unspeakable toilets; taking showers in the streets and buying honey and watermelons to keep ourselves going, trying to act like tourists.

From Morocco we flew back to Heathrow. The fear never went, even once we were outside Libya. The sight of the British officials at the airport made my stomach turn as badly as the actual snatch had done.

Every mission was different. On one I was smuggling my sister-in-law's son out of Iraq for her because she was living in England and they couldn't get the child out. I had to use my son's passport for him, but the boy looked very different from my son: to begin with, my son had blond hair and blue eyes while this boy had black hair and eyes. So I had to sedate him with Valium, terrified that I might get the dosage wrong and make him sick. I then shaved off his hair and his eyebrows and told the officials that my son was dying of leukaemia and was undergoing chemotherapy.

When we finally reached Heathrow he woke up and started running around wanting to go the toilet. In my terror I completely lost the ability to speak Arabic. The officials became concerned and asked if I was okay. I changed my tack and became aggressive, telling them what a dreadful flight I'd had and what a monster the child had been. They took pity, stamped the passport and found a porter for me. I was terrified they would come through into the airport with me and his mum would be waiting for him, blowing my story to pieces. I'd spent weeks teaching him to behave like an English child, calling me Mum and feeding himself rather than making the adults do it for him as had been happening with his relatives. That particular trip nearly put me off the rescue business for good. Coupled with the stress, spending 17 days in the heat of Iraq with no air conditioning had left me drained and sick.

It had been a harrowing rescue all the way. At Jordan airport, on my way to London, they'd called my name out over the tannoy and I was sure I'd been found out. There were police everywhere, but they just wanted me to pay a fine for overstaying my visa. They had also noticed that my daughter – whom I'd taken with me – and I had stamps in our passports saying we'd gone into Iraq, while my 'son' only had one out of Iraq into Jordan. I had to do some fast talking to get out of that one.

After I'd done the first rescue, Mary talked about me around the area and a number of women started to approach me at places like the school gates asking me for help. I would take their numbers and promise to call them. I found it impossible to say no to any of them, and I ended up with 400-pound phone bills every quarter. I never charged anyone any money; they just had to find enough to pay for the expenses involved in the trip. My long-suffering husband, Mohammed, was enormously supportive and I wouldn't have been able to do any of it had I not felt confident about leaving the children in his care, sometimes for several weeks at a time.

The second rescue was in Morocco. The child was a similar age to Leila. The victims nearly always seem to be about five or six years old; that is when the Muslim men start to panic about their children being brought up in a western culture. I've never been asked to rescue a baby, and I doubt if it would be possible. But the men don't want to take them when they're very tiny, anyway. At that stage they don't mind what country they're being brought up in, and looking after them without their mothers there is too hard anyway. So they wait until the children are a little independent but still young enough to follow their fathers trustingly wherever they take them.

This child had been spotted by a friend of the mother at a Moroccan holiday resort, so we had to move quickly – before their holiday ended and they went back to whichever address she had been hidden at. Speed is never a problem. If necessary I can plan a trip and get to the destination within a day.

Once there, the mother and I booked into a hotel in the resort and actually spotted the child from our balcony. We watched from a distance and then I got talking to the child's grandmother on the beach. It was a nice family and the child was playing happily with the others; there was no question that she was being maltreated, but I still believed that a child should, in almost every instance, be with its mother.

We waited until the grandmother and aunt went off to buy some sandwiches and then the mother lifted her veil and showed herself to her daughter. She took the girl's hand and they walked off down the beach towards the car that we had waiting. I lingered a moment or two until the women came back from the sandwich bar, saw that the child was gone and started to panic. They were scouring the sea, imagining she must have drowned. They weren't taking any notice of me, so I slipped away and joined the mother and child at the hotel. We had a flight booked for that day and it looked as if we would be able to make it. With the adrenaline pumping we made the flight with 45 minutes to spare; the last ones onto the plane.

Over the last three years I've built up something of a support network in the Middle East. I have drivers in most of the countries, whom I've kept in touch with and whom I trust; men who know what I do and believe it's right that children should be allowed to stay with their mothers. I also have officials I can go to sometimes for advice and help, and I know how to talk to them. The women that I help have none of this, which means they don't know where to start on their own. Sometimes I can find out by telephoning from England where the children are at school, which makes the planning much easier. It's amazing how much information people will give you over the phone, even senior government people.

My first experience of escaping with a child was with my own son from my first marriage. My husband was half Cypriot and half Saudi. He was a good man but I was too young to be married. I became so bored in Cyprus with nothing to do that I realised quite soon I'd made a mistake. I wanted to go back to England, but the family made it clear that if I did, I would be leaving my son behind. There was no way I was going to do that, so I had to plan our escape thoroughly.

Things seldom went as planned on any of the rescues. On one trip in Egypt the child in question was living in a flat and not going to school, so the mother and I had to change our method of operation. In Egypt, people have a habit of sharing taxis. We waited outside the block in a cab and when the grandmother came out with the child we followed her down the road until she hailed our driver.

The mother of the child was sitting in the front passenger seat, her face covered, and I was in the back with them. The child was squashed between me and the grandmother, a huge woman who filled more than her share of the seat. My heart was thumping so loudly I was sure she must be able to hear it. When we got to our destination the grandmother got out. As she fumbled for her money I held onto the child and ordered the driver to go, pulling the door shut as we sped away into the traffic. Horns were honking all around us, making our nerves jangle even more.

Looking back I could see the grandmother shouting and waving her fists at us. It occurred to me she might have taken the taxi's number so we changed cars as soon as we were out of sight. The new taxi took us back to our hotel room at the Marriott and while I packed our few belongings the mother went downstairs and paid the bill. I'm always surprised how quickly the children adapt from being scared to being content to be with their mothers, wherever they might be taking them. I didn't think it was safe to go to the airport and so we caught a boat to Cyprus and flew back to Heathrow the next day.

I was back in Egypt a few months later looking for a ten-year-old boy who'd been taken three months before. I felt there was something wrong about the set-up but I couldn't put my finger on what it was. I noticed that when the mother rang to speak to the child he didn't want to talk to her. It didn't seem as if he had been away long enough for them to be able to brainwash him to that extent. But she managed to convince me and so I put my doubts to one side and set out on the mission alone.

I phoned the driver we had used before and he met me from the airport. He took me to stay with his family, which was nice. We followed the boy and his grandparents to an Arabic cabaret nightclub and went in with my driver friend and his wife. We managed to get seats at a table next to the family and I fell into conversation with the boy when I heard him speaking English. The grandmother asked me where I was from and when I said London she told me the boy's mother was from there.

'That's nice,' I said cheerfully.

'No,' she shook her head. 'Very bad woman. She beat him badly with many things.' She told the boy to roll up his sleeves and show me the cigarette burns.

'Do you miss your Mum?' I asked him.

'No,' he said, 'I don't like my mother.'

'You're saying that because you're with your Dad,' I teased him. 'And because you love your grandma, don't you?'

'No,' he said, without a smile. 'I don't want to see my mother ever again. I asked my father to bring me here to my grandmother.'

That night I rang the mother and told her I wasn't bringing him back. She went mad, reminding me she'd paid for my fare. Even if I'd wanted to take him, how would I have dragged a ten-year-old boy to the airport if he didn't want to go? The whole idea was ridiculous and I wished I'd trusted my instincts in the first place.

'I'll give you the fare money back,' I said, 'But I'm not bringing the boy back to you.'

When I got back to England I refunded her the expenses out of my own pocket. I didn't want her accusing me of taking her money under false pretences. She still went round telling people I'd let her down.

The most frightening country to rescue children from was Turkey. It may just have been because I'd seen the film *Midnight Express* so I knew what would be in store for me if I were caught. I had to find a seven-year-old on a beach in Marmaris, amongst hundreds of other kids. Initially I went alone because the mother couldn't afford two tickets, but when I got there I wasn't able to find the child. The mother had to come out to join me and we searched for a week before we eventually located the little girl back in Istanbul. We grabbed her while she was playing outside with other children. There were police everywhere and I knew that word would get out quickly in Turkey, so we drove across the desert to Kurdistan and on to Iraq and Jordan. At every police stop I was sure the game was up and we were about to be arrested as they checked our papers and then looked around the car as if searching for something.

Sometimes the mothers lose control of themselves when they see their kids again for the first time. One of them, on a mission to Morocco, completely ignored my warnings and ran over and grabbed her child the moment we saw him. It was nearly a disaster, with us being chased down the street by the women. It was very unfair on the child who was deeply shocked and frightened by the chase.

In 2002 Sarra Fotheringham asked me to travel with her to Dubai to help her rescue her son, Tariq, from his father's family. What I didn't realise was that Sarra's new husband in England was selling his story to the papers and that this was tipping off the authorities in Dubai. We managed to reach Tariq, but as we prepared to get on a boat out of the country with him the police swooped and we were arrested. The prosecutor wanted to make an example of us. We were put straight into jail, sharing with 70 other women. A few days later we were bailed out but told we must stay in the country for trial. It didn't look as if I was going to be able to avoid a long prison sentence, until one of the most powerful sheikhs in the land gave me permission to leave. My picture has now been all over the papers and it'll be harder for me to work under cover, but I shall continue to help women to get their children back in any way I can.

As well as being an adventure story, I want this book to be of genuine help to women who are in danger of losing their children. I want to show them how to see the danger signs and tell them what they should do to protect themselves and their sons and daughters, so that they never have to resort to coming to someone like me for assistance.

ENDS

This synopsis was then followed by a chapter breakdown. Although the eventual order of the chapters was different when we actually came to write the book, the essence was the same and the publisher was able to see that there would be enough material for a whole book and that it wouldn't simply be one adventure listed after another. We showed that the reader would see into Donya's past and grow to understand why she took the risks she did and what had caused her to take up such a dangerous life at the same time as being caught up in the stake-outs, snatches and car chases across the desert. For the chapter breakdown I reverted to the third person.

Chapter Breakdown

CHAPTER ONE. OUT OF IRAQ.

The story opens with the dramatic escape from Iraq with Donya's little nephew. The reader is immediately caught by the tension and the excitement of getting the child across the Iraqi border and out of Jordan to England. Donya then explains how she's spent the previous three weeks in the blistering heat of Iraq teaching the five-year-old boy how to behave as if he is her son, changing his appearance to fit the passport photograph and planning the actual escape. By the time they arrive back at Heathrow the reader is hooked on the excitement and wants to know more about Donya herself and how she came to be on such a dangerous mission.

CHAPTER TWO. A MOTHER'S PLEA.

Going back a couple of years, Donya explains how she met Mary at a bus stop in Queensway and realised that she had to do something to help. She tells how she found herself volunteering to go into Libya and save the child for her new friend, and describes the desperation and helplessness which women like Mary feel when their children are taken away from them. She then takes the reader on the first rescue mission, to get Leila back from Libya, hooking them once more on the excitement of the long trip back to safety via Algeria and Morocco.

CHAPTER THREE. BECOMING A MUSLIM.

In this chapter Donya describes how she came to be converted to the Muslim religion at the age of 16. She gives a moving account of her own troubled childhood and how she found an escape through the family of her first boyfriend in Jordan. She paints a vivid picture of what it was like for a 15-year-old English girl to find herself part of a Muslim family and what it was about the lifestyle and the religion that attracted her.

CHAPTER FOUR. BECOMING THE SCARLET PIMPERNEL.

After rescuing Leila, word spreads around the West London Muslim community that Donya is someone who can help mothers in distress. In this chapter she tells of the many women who approached her asking for help, explaining the pattern which started to emerge for her from their stories; how all the women had had similar experiences. In describing how these situations arise, she'll be able to help other women in mixed marriages to spot the danger signals and suggest ways in which they can protect themselves and their children from being separated. She ends the chapter by describing how she heard that an abducted child had been spotted at a holiday resort in Morocco, and gives a gripping account of how she and the child's mother took it back from the family on the beach.

CHAPTER FIVE. MY OWN FIRST ESCAPE.

In this chapter Donya talks about how as a teenager she got herself into trouble in Tunisia, where she was engaged to be married, and how she ran away on her wedding day – going into hiding and having to enlist her mother's help to get back to England without a passport. She goes on to tell the exciting story of a later rescue from Egypt where she and the mother had to lure a child and its grandmother into their taxi in order to escape back home via Cyprus.

CHAPTER SIX. MISBEHAVING.

Not wanting to hold herself up as any sort of saint, whatever the women she helps may think of her, Donya will be brutally honest about her own indiscretions. In this chapter she tells of how she met a Saudi millionaire and lived in luxury with him in Park Lane, travelling to all the most exotic holiday locations. By describing the lifestyle, she gives another insight into why so many western girls are dazzled by Muslim men with their apparent wealth and exciting lives. She also shows how the relationship started to go wrong and how she took her revenge by running up £750,000 worth of bills on his American Express card – a fantasy many women must have harboured at one time or another.

CHAPTER SEVEN. BECOMING A MOTHER.

When she married a wealthy Cypriot and moved to Cyprus, Donya learnt two valuable lessons. Firstly she learnt about the bond between a mother and a child, when she gave birth to her first son. She then learnt how frightening it is to think that you might lose contact with a child because of a breakdown in the marital relationship. She tells how she realised she didn't want to spend her life as a pampered wife, waiting at home for her husband to get back from work, and how she made sure she didn't lose her son when she left the marriage. From that moment on she was never in any doubt that children who wish to remain with their mothers should be allowed to do so.

She's also anxious to demonstrate that she's not against men simply because of their gender; that sometimes she knows a child is better off with its father than its mother. She tells the story of the little boy in Egypt whom the mother asked her to rescue, but whom she realised had been abused when he was in England and consequently needed to stay in Egypt with his father.

CHAPTER EIGHT. COPING WITH THE FEAR.

Donya has to face two kinds of fear in her life. The first is the fear that many women in mixed marriages have to face constantly, that they will wake up one morning and find their children have been taken away from them. In this chapter she will provide some golden rules for women in this situation to help them protect themselves and their children and make their lives more tolerable.

For herself she also has to face the adrenalin-pumping experiences of the actual snatches and the escapes that sometimes take days, as she crosses international borders and braves checkpoints and police searches along the way. In this chapter she'll remember some of the most frightening moments from the last three years, particularly in Turkey.

CHAPTER NINE. A HAPPY MARRIAGE.

When Donya met Mohammed she'd finally found the man she wanted to spend the rest of her life with. Still a devout Muslim, she knew she wanted to marry a Muslim man, but he had to be someone she could trust, and someone who would help and support her in whatever she chose to do with her life. She and Mohammed have three children themselves, as well as bringing up her son from her first marriage, and he supports her completely in the work she does rescuing children for other, less empowered women, looking after the children when she is away on missions. In this chapter she'll describe a partnership that works, despite the cultural divides, and how they've coped together with her growing notoriety, both in the local community and in the national media, as a modern Scarlet Pimpernel.

CHAPTER TEN. THE COVER BLOWN.

When Sarra Fotheringham asked Donya to go to Dubai with her to bring back her son, Tariq, it seemed a relatively straight-forward mission. What she didn't realise was that Sarra's new husband in England was in the process of selling his story to the media. The authorities in Dubai were alerted and, as the two women boarded a boat to escape the country with Tariq, they swooped and arrested them.

The public prosecutor was determined to make an example of them, particularly Donya. After several days in jail, sharing a toilet with 70 other women, they were released on bail, but still couldn't leave the country until they had faced trial. It was only after a chance meeting with one of the most powerful Sheikhs in the country that they were able to get permission to leave.

The British media had plastered Donya's real name and picture all over their pages. Her cover was blown and it will be hard to undertake any more missions personally. But she is still determined to keep up the fight to reunite women with their children when they have been unfairly parted.

This chapter will tell the exciting story of the arrest and how it felt to have a prison sentence in a foreign land hanging over her head as she desperately tried to find a way to get home to her husband and children.

ENDS

This next example had the advantage of having the cachet of Greenpeace attached to it, but at the same time we had to demonstrate just what an interesting individual David McTaggart was. We could afford to go into more detail on the opening pages because we could be confident that any publisher receiving this document would be certain to want to read it. In that way it was an easier sell, but the agent involved was also going to be looking for a lot of money for such an important world figure, so we had to make sure the publishers understood just what a good read it would be and how they would be sure to recoup their outlay.

THE AUTOBIOGRAPHY OF DAVID MCTAGGART

The Author

David McTaggart is a maverick who has built a movement of five million people – a movement that has fought governments and won, saved a continent and changed the way in which everyone thinks about the future of the planet.

During his 25 years creating and running Greenpeace International he's remained an enigma, shying away from personal media exposure, developing a reputation amongst world leaders as a man who can be trusted to be discreet, a man they can do business with.

In 1969 an explosion in a ski lodge in California changed David McTaggart's life. He was in his mid-30s and had already made and lost several fortunes in the construction business. This time, however, he decided it was time to follow a different path.

After a year of hedonism in Tahiti he bought Vega, a 38-foot ketch, and set off to live a vagabond life, sailing amongst the islands and atolls of the South Pacific, enjoying the freedom of the open seas where no man could tell him what to do or where to go. He was happy with his new lifestyle.

When the French Government announced their intention to detonate nuclear bombs in the international waters surrounding Muroroa atoll, they told the sailors in the area that they must stay outside the 120-mile 'exclusion zone'.

McTaggart took exception to this invasion of his freedom

and decided to make a stand by sailing Vega into the zone and refusing to move. From that tiny beginning grew the Greenpeace movement, which was to prove the bane of many a government and international corporation's life. The movement eventually succeeded in stopping the nuclear testing and alerting the world to the dangers of dumping nuclear waste. It succeeded in saving Antartica from oil and mineral exploitation and in rescuing countless species of whales from extinction.

While the trials and tribulations of the organisation and its famous ship, Rainbow Warrior, were constantly in the headlines, McTaggart deliberately kept out of the limelight – only occasionally, reluctantly, allowing profiles of himself to appear in international media like *Time*. By acquiring a reputation for being discreet he was able to gain access to the highest levels of government and big business all over the world, and given unrivalled insights into who was actually running the planet and who was destroying it.

His global network of contacts included names as varied as Mikhail Gorbachev and Jimmy Carter, Ted Turner and Pierre Trudeau, Rajiv Gandhi and Bryan Adams, Chancellor Kohl and Sir Peter Scott.

In his career as an environmentalist he has received the Onassis Prize, the Kreisky Prize in Austria, the UN Global 500 Award, the Order of the Golden Arch given by the King of the Netherlands, the RSPCA Award in Britain, the Better World Society Award, the German Golden Camera Award, the Italian Zolfanello d'Oro, the Colomba D'Ora Peace Prize and the Green Life Award.

Although still highly active in the international arena, McTaggart retired as Chairman and Executive Director of Greenpeace in 1991. In 1995 he staged his own disappearance in the South Pacific when the French announced that they were re-starting nuclear testing, drawing the attention of virtually all the world's media to the problem and causing an international outcry which halted the testing.

He continues to serve as Greenpeace's Honorary Chair, and now lives in Umbria, on an idyllic farm where he produces the best olive oil in the world and has a little time to reflect on the last 25 years and what is likely to happen in the next millenium.

The Book

This book lifts the curtain on the secretive world of global politics and our environment. No one has ever achieved such unrivalled access to so many of the rooms where the decisions affecting our future are made. McTaggart has been involved in the deals and the trade-offs, the pressure groups and the think-tanks which have determined the sort of world we live in.

From the ice flows of Antarctica to the paradise islands of the South Pacific, from the homes of Western billionaires to those of communist leaders, he's dealt with everyone from the Presidents of super-powers to the Mafia, from media moguls to armed commandos. They've hunted him, attacked him, tried to intimidate and discredit him, but have been unable to stop him.

McTaggart will explain how he built a world-wide movement, growing it at a rate of 35% a year ending up with 1000 employees, five million members, an annual income of £100-million and an unrivalled intelligence network of computer hackers. He will explain the convictions that drove him to give up his sybaritic life in the South Pacific to challenge the governments of some of the most powerful nations on earth. He will tell of the horrors he saw, the conspiracies he uncovered and the adventures he enjoyed in his battles to make the planet safe for our children.

In recounting the stories and the intrigues he will reveal just who has the power to save us or destroy us; who has made billions from exploiting the planet; and who has flagrantly broken international laws and codes of practice in order to keep the money flowing into their pockets.

This will be the definitive book on *the* environmental movement of the last 25 years, backed by the copious Greenpeace files and McTaggart's international network of contacts.

Despite the many victories that Greenpeace has achieved, we're still in danger of destroying our habitat – perhaps even more so than 25 years ago:

- We are still using too much energy and creating too much pollution.
- Most of the world is now facing shortages of fresh water and the situation is worsening every year.

- There is a growth in nuclear testing to modernise arsenals and create new weapons.
- The conventional arms race is now on again, with the Americans, Britons and Russians leading the market, draining international financial resources and increasing regional tensions.
- The destruction of tropical and boreal forests is leading to a loss of species, a destruction of bio-diversity and increasing the threat of genetic engineering as we lose our biological patrimony.
- The world's supply of fish is being wiped out without regard for quotas, which will lead to enormous food problems.
- The multinational companies are becoming more and more powerful, threatening democracy and making it impossible to undertake the changes needed to safe-guard our environment.

This book will tell the shocking facts of what is still going wrong behind the scenes and being covered up by vested interests, and suggest what we can do about it.

ENDS

There was then an extensive chapter breakdown. Although I had been commissioned to write the synopsis, the actual writing of the book was done by another ghost.

What a synopsis has to do:

The first page has to make the publisher want to read more.

It has to show how interesting the material is.

It has to demonstrate how the book will be written.

It has to convince the publishers that there is enough for a complete book.

It has to make both the book and the author seem easy to promote and market.

9

Getting the Job Done

So far I have concentrated on how to get the ghosting work in the first place, and how to sell projects to publishers successfully. Now we need to think about what it will take to actually get the books created.

The first step has to be to find the subject, or to make yourself available for someone to approach you, using the methods discussed in chapter 4. When you have found a possible subject you need to ascertain whether there is going to be enough material for a whole book. The ideal situation is to find that out before you invest time in meeting them.

Background material

There may be some written material in existence – either in the form of background material, or a first draft of the book that the subject may have tried to write before realising that they needed professional help. Encourage the subject to supply you with everything that exists. They may be reluctant, being self-conscious about their spelling or their writing style. Assure them that this is of no importance because you will be sorting all that side of things out in due course. If possible, read the material before you meet them so that you have a better idea of what questions to ask. If they are hesitant to send you confidential material, offer to sign a confidentiality agreement as discussed in chapter 6.

Sometimes an author will have managed to sell their idea to a publisher and will initially have felt confident they could manage the manuscript themselves. They then find themselves with so much written material that they can't work out how to put it in order. Gerald O'Farrell had spent 30 years researching and writing about Ancient Egypt when he came up with a theory that Howard Carter and Lord Carnarvon had invented the story about discovering Tutankhamun's tomb and had, in fact, been plundering it for years before they finally announced its discovery to the world. Gerald had amassed so much information and research material, and had so many theories in his head, that he couldn't see how to distil it all down to a digestible story that the publishers could present to the reading public. I was able to bring a fresh eye to the subject. It was an entertaining theory and I was able to see which bits of his research built his case and which were merely distractions. The mountains of material he had assembled, coupled with a few days of interviewing, provided me with about ten times as much information as I needed. The job was then to give it shape and speed so that the reader had time to breathe and understand. The resulting *Tutankhamun Deception* was a controversial but highly readable book. People might have argued with Gerald's theories, but at least they were able to follow them and see how he had come to them.

Similarly, when Helen Attwater wanted to write about her experiences with her husband running an orphanage for baby gorillas in the Congo, she had so much information she didn't know where to start. Not only was it a story of life with 50 or more of the most endearing animals in the world, it was also a story of survival through incredible adversity, fighting illness and surviving in a bloody civil war as they struggled to re-introduce the gorillas into the wild. The amount of material she had managed to amass on her return from the nightmare was awe-inspiring, but there was far too much for any reader to be able to digest. It was one of the most moving and uplifting stories imaginable, and it wasn't hard for me as a ghost to find enough material to make a stunning and gripping narrative for *My Gorilla Journey*.

Not many would-be authors have this much existing material to give to a ghost – and some have nothing on record at all, in which case you will need to coax the basic facts of the story out of them as early in the relationship as possible in order to ascertain whether you are going to be able to help them.

Some authors may find it easier to communicate with you via e-mail in the first instance, in order to give you the bare bones of the story.

And some people, particularly if they live a great distance from you, may be happy putting the initial story onto tape. They may be more comfortable talking into a microphone than they would be tapping away at a keyboard. This can be a very useful way for you to get an idea of their voice and whether it is something that can be sustained for a whole book. If you can see from the beginning that it is not something you will be able to sell to publishers, then you need to be honest. It is much worse for both of you if you 'umm' and 'aah' about it when you already know that it is a non-starter. The difficulty here, of course, is that it is sometimes hard to predict which stories will work until you have tried; but there are some which you know, from the first moment, are not suitable for book form.

Telling people the bad news

It is always hard telling people that they don't have enough material for a whole book. Often it is their whole lives you are dismissing in this one sentence. If you explain, however, just how hard it is to get books published, and that no ghost can afford to spend months working speculatively on a project unless a publisher can be persuaded to pay an advance, they will nearly always understand. They may tell you you're wrong, and you will have to admit that that is a possibility. It is also possible that their story could make a newspaper or magazine feature, even if it isn't enough for a whole book.

If they insist on a meeting as the first step, before giving you any information, you have to assess whether you think it is a gamble worth taking. Provided that there aren't too many travel expenses involved, it will only cost you time. If you are not too busy then it might not be worth setting up a speculative meeting. If you're just starting out then any lead is worth following up.

Zana Muhsen was very reluctant to tell me anything over the phone when she first contacted me, and I had to decide whether it was worth buying a train ticket from Sussex to Birmingham in order to meet her. The fact that the resulting book has sold millions of copies shows that it is sometimes worth taking a gamble. Equally, I have travelled enormous distances and incurred horrible expenses to meet people who sounded certain on the phone that they had a story that would set the publishing and film worlds into a spin, but didn't.

It can be even harder to tell these hopeful authors that their story is unlikely to find a publisher once you have actually met them. By that time you have already formed a relationship and listened sympathetically to what they have to say. The only way to break the news is to put it very practically: for example, 'You have obviously been through a great deal, but I just don't think I will be able to persuade a publisher to pay enough money to make writing it viable,' or 'You are obviously absolutely expert in this subject, but I know there are already books in the market on the subject and I don't believe publishers will be willing to pay enough to back another one.'

No matter how you do it, though, it is always difficult; once you've done it a few times you will find yourself becoming much more sympathetic towards publishers and agents who have to issue streams of rejections on a daily basis.

Where to meet

If you decide to meet the would-be author, then you have to suggest the best place. I think it is always better to meet them on their own home territory if possible. You will get a much better idea of who they are and what their tastes are if you get to see their home, or at least their office. You might even get to meet partners or colleagues who are relevant to the story. They will also be far more relaxed if you are the guest than if they come to your house. The idea is to make them as comfortable as possible, and to make the whole process of writing the book as pleasant and easy for them as you can – starting at the first meeting.

If they insist on coming to see you at your house then they may just want to set their minds at rest about you. They want to see that you are trustworthy, and they may feel better if they know where they will be able to find you later. Subjects are very nervous when they first meet a ghostwriter, even though they won't admit it until later. They're desperate to make a good impression because they know that the final outcome of the book will depend to an extent on the initial impressions the ghost goes away with. So the first job is to make them aware that the book can be whatever they want it to be; that the ghost will advise on what they think is the best way to win a publisher and get the story across to the reading public, but that ultimately *they* are the customer and they are always right. Once they realise that, they will begin to relax.

If they don't want you to go to their home then it might be an idea to arrange a neutral location. Large hotel lobbies are good because you can then order coffee or move on to a meal if the meeting goes well and you both want to prolong it. If they're nervous about other people overhearing what they have to say then you can always hire a private room, although you need to establish who is going to be paying for anything like that at this stage.

If you are going to be using tape recording equipment (see pp. 109–110) you will need to be somewhere quiet and away from other people if possible. If you can't go to their home, either because they don't want people to know they are writing a book, or because it is too noisy or distracting, then hotel rooms are very useful. You're probably only going to need two or three days of intensive interviewing in most cases, so the costs shouldn't spiral too far out of hand unless you choose a very expensive location. On several occasions I have travelled to the author's hometown, ensconced myself in a hotel room for a weekend, and invited them to come in and talk for as many hours as they want to. That way I can also visit their home and meet anyone they want me to meet, while having somewhere private and quiet in which to record and allow them to unburden themselves.

If the subjects are wealthy and in a position to be hospitable you may end up spending a very pleasant few days as their guests. In recent years I have found myself in a millionaire's ski chalet in the Swiss Alps, a chateau in the South of France and a Bermuda beach house. I have also spent time in an orphanage in a war zone, a primitive Chinese village and hotels everywhere from Kuala Lumpur to Birmingham, Juan les Pins to Hollywood. The variety, of course, is part of the excitement and part of what, hopefully, makes each book sound and feel different.

One advantage of meeting a subject in your own home, of course, is that they have to take the time and expense to travel. The disadvantage is that you, as the host, have to feed and accommodate them if that is appropriate. On their own territory, you can call it a day and leave whenever you feel that you need a break. Etiquette makes it much harder to call for a break in your own house.

Research

As I explained in chapter 1, one of the great advantages of ghosting is that you don't have to spend a great deal of time on research, because your author already knows all about the subject. You can write about their nightmare experiences in the darkest parts of the Congo without actually having to risk life and limb yourself. If there is some aspect of the country or culture that you are not sure about, you simply ask them and they will give you their view, which is the one you want; if you can't picture a scene then you can ask them to describe it in their own words.

You may sometimes feel the need to verify facts your subject has given you, or to follow up something they are vague about. In most cases, however, they should be able to provide you with everything you need. (See pp. 108–9 for more information on what to do if you suspect that they are 'lying' to you, and pp. 58–60 on how to protect yourself from possible legal repercussions in your initial contract.)

It can also, however, be useful to visit the places in which books are set, to experience them for yourself. I ghosted *A Promise of Hope* for Mark Cook, a Gurkha Colonel who had built an orphanage in Croatia at the time when ethnic cleansing in that region was at its height, and then gone on to found the enormously successful Hope and Homes for Children charity. Although Mark was able to give me a good description of Croatia and of how it felt to change his career path so radically in mid-life, it was also enormously helpful to actually be able to stay in the orphanage and live amongst the children for a while; to see the bombed-out buildings at first-hand and to experience the hardships that the local population were undergoing. You can conjure more vivid and colourful images on the page when you have seen them for yourself. I was also able to see the Colonel in the setting of the book; to see his rapport with the children and with the other people who assisted with the building. It helped when it came to catching his voice and reliving the experience with him. Without actually meeting the children in the orphanage for myself it would have been hard to depict the different characters of those who had impinged on Mark's consciousness during the adventure.

Similarly, when writing about Tan Sri Loy – a Chinese billionaire living in Malaysia – it helped to actually see the village that he had come from and to meet his relatives. The Chinese culture is very different from anything we might experience in Europe, and there were extraordinary things about his background that he would have taken for granted and not mentioned if I hadn't seen them for myself.

When I was writing *Heroine of the Desert* for Donya Al-Nahi, I found it easier to build a picture of the area in London where she lived, and where she met most of the women whose children had been snatched, by actually walking around and drinking in the atmosphere. That way I was able to put some local colour into the opening pages before plunging into the action with all its car chases, stake-outs, kidnappings and shootings. Here are the opening paragraphs:

The whole adventure was started by a polite conversation with a stranger at a bus stop in Queensway on a warm, damp day in 1998. The stop is outside Whiteley's shopping centre, a place where I was going to be sitting for many hours and hearing a great many shocking and heart-breaking stories in the coming years.

Queensway is one of those 'melting pot' areas of London: a long road with one end touching the north border of Hyde Park, just a short walk from Kensington Palace and some of the biggest and most expensive houses in London. At the other end lies Westbourne Grove and all around live people of every race that has ever made London its home, stretching up to the West-Indian-dominated areas of Ladbroke Grove and across to Maida Vale and Kilburn. Tens of thousands of families of widely differing incomes and lifestyles live in a hotch-potch of flats and houses, some grand and others cramped and cheaply subdivided in order to contain far more people than the original architects ever envisaged.

On one side of this sector lies the West End with all its tourist and entertainment delights, and on the other, Notting Hill is fast changing from being bohemian and ethnic to becoming almost as wealthy and fashionable as the West End residential addresses. South of us lie the wide green acres of Hyde Park and north of us sprawl the endless anonymous suburbs of outer London.

Queensway itself has an endearing scruffiness about it and is dominated by shops and restaurants with an Arab flavour. Small grocery stores stand open to the street with their fruit and vegetables piled high on display, the insides of the shops crammed floor to ceiling with unexpected choices of products. Whole families often seem to be serving the customers or talking animatedly to one another when there are no customers. There's a temporary feel about the place, as if many of the residents and businesses are only passing through, making ends meet while they're here, laying plans to return to their homelands or move on to better things. The people may come from a wide range of different countries, but the feel of the place is simply Middle Eastern, from the sounds of the voices to the smells of the cooking, from the Arabic shop signs to the women's headdresses and the music seeping from the shops and restaurants on warm days. It's an area I know well and feel comfortable with. It's the area that has become my home.

It is perfectly possible to write a book for someone, having done nothing but listen to their words; but extra research often helps to provide more material and descriptive ideas. It can also suggest other questions that you can ask of the subject.

It is important, however, not to shoehorn-in extra research just to pad out the text, if it isn't strictly relevant to the story. Croatia has a long and terrible history which I could easily have researched in some detail and inserted into the book, but the information would not have sat easily alongside the very immediate thoughts, experiences and emotions that Mark Cook wanted to put into his book. There were elements of Malaysian history, however, that had happened during Tan Sri Loy's lifetime that had a great influence on how he managed to build his company and his fortune. He didn't have the time to give me a complete history of the country over the previous 60 years, and so some judicious reading and interviewing of other people helped me to know what to ask him when he was able to see me.

There are times when the main subject of the book has trouble thinking of enough things to say. It is then useful to talk to friends and relatives in order to get stories and references that you can use to jog the author's memory. Questions such as, 'Your mother remembers a time when you used to sleep with everyone who asked ...', or 'Your brother says you never did an honest day's work in your life,' or 'I was told you made over a million dollars in one night from a deal involving a fake Picasso,' will all elicit interesting responses.

What if they 'lie' to you?

'Lie' is probably too strong a word. Most of us tend to embroider our memories to suit the picture of ourselves that we would like the world to see. We want to forget about the menial jobs we had to do on our rise to the top, or the relationships in which we didn't behave quite as well as we would have liked, or the wilderness years when nothing much happened because we were still living at home with our mums. We want to seem funnier, sexier, more exciting or more interesting than we are – and anyone with a large enough ego to want to write a book is unlikely to be exempt from this failing.

There may be occasions, therefore, on which the subject will tell the ghost something that contradicts something else they have said, or something that the ghost already knows about them. If that happens it is important to mention it immediately; not as any sort of accusation, but merely as a point of interest. 'Yesterday you said you were still in Burma in 1953, and now you're saying you were in Hong Kong all through the 50s. We really need to get the dates straight.' Or, 'I think the reader may be confused here, because you say you've never done anything wrong in your life, and yet you've served half a dozen prison sentences for a variety of crimes. We really need to clarify what we're saying...' You get the picture.

If they have actually failed to convince you that they have got their story straight, then you must tell them – because if *you* aren't convinced by what they are saying, you will have difficulty convincing the readers. If they can put up a reasoned argument for why every one of their prison sentences was a travesty of justice, then you will be able to reproduce their arguments equally convincingly, but they do have to be made to justify themselves and everything they say.

If, when you hand in the manuscript, the publisher doesn't believe what they are reading, then it is between them and the author. The ghost can honestly hold up his or her hands and disclaim all responsibility. Your job is to produce the books that the authors would have written themselves if they had been able and willing. If they would have said those things in the book themselves, then the ghost should also put them in, having made every effort to make them convincing to the reader.

Recording equipment

You do need to record most authors at some length. You simply won't be able to remember an entire book's worth of material, however carefully you listen, and taking the whole thing down in shorthand is probably asking the impossible of virtually anyone who isn't a top-of-the-range trained secretary.

Tape recorders, however, can be intimidating for people who aren't used to them. Even celebrities who are experienced in giving interviews will become more guarded in their words if they know they are being recorded. Assure them from the start that no one except you will ever listen to the tapes, and promise to let them have them at the end of the writing process if they want them. In my experience people seldom ask for the tapes in the end, because by that time you have gained their trust, and you can then clean them and use them again.

The recorder itself needs to be as small and discreet as possible so that they tend to forget about it. I use small, office Dictaphones, which will just sit on the arm of the author's chair or on a nearby table. I prefer them to be battery-driven, as I don't want to be restricted to finding a power-point to run them from. I would rather the author was in their most comfortable seat and then I can just put the recorder as near to them as possible. I use a more powerful desktop machine to play the tapes back later in order to get a better sound quality.

Always put in new batteries before you start a session. There is nothing worse than discovering that the machine has run down without you noticing and you have missed hours, or even minutes, of interesting material. And if you buy a new machine, practise with it beforehand so that you are completely familiar with the controls. You do not want to be fiddling with buttons and having to think about the mechanics of the thing at the moment when you should be concentrating on your questions.

I find it very useful to have a notebook and pen at the same time, so that if a question occurs to me while the author is in full flow I can jot it down and carry on listening to them without interrupting – and without having to worry about forgetting the question. It is also quite useful to have something to look at from time to time, so that you aren't staring too hard at the subject. While you do need to demonstrate that you are enthralled by what they are saying, they may become a little nervous if you are staring at them too ferociously. Looking down at a notepad breaks that eye contact, whereas looking around at anything else may make it seem as if your attention is wandering.

How much tape you need will depend on how concisely the author talks. If they wander around the point a lot and you have difficulty getting them back on track, you will need to spend far more time extracting the information. If they are pretty concise you probably don't need more than 20 hours, particularly if there are other sources of information like manuscripts to consult. You will know that you have done as much recording as necessary when you have run out of questions to ask.

The questions

In order to know what questions you need to ask, you have to picture yourself sitting down to write the book. What do you need to know? Once you have a rough idea in your head of how you will be structuring the story, it becomes obvious what to ask.

If the book is a narrative, rather than a 'how-to' book, keep them talking chronologically. This will improve your understanding of the facts, and of the author's likely state of mind at any given time in the story – as well as making it easier for you to sort through your notes and tapes at a later date. It may well be that you will play around with the timeframe of the story once you have the whole picture: publishers often want the most exciting part to come first anyway. I wrote a book called *Nowhere to Hide* for an English lady called Susan Francis, who had married an Iraqi and was living in Baghdad when the Allied Forces attacked in 1991. After enduring the bombing with her family in a shelter, she fled with them into the Kurdish mountains, just as the bombing stopped and Saddam Hussein turned on the Kurds.

The book covered Susan's whole life, but rather than beginning with her childhood, we started it as dramatically as possible. The following was the opening paragraph:

> It was our wedding anniversary, and it seemed as if we were now going to die together, slow, agonising deaths with our grandsons in our arms. Or, worse still, Azziz would go first, leaving me alone to look after the children on the mountain, a task I was now too weak to manage on my own. I walked outside in the chilly dawn rain, while Azziz and the two boys, too feeble to rouse themselves, slept in the car, which had run out of petrol days before. I didn't even have enough supplies left to make a pot of tea to warm their sick stomachs. Hunger and thirst were gnawing at our insides, the pain mixing with the diseases and poisons that were now gripping us all.

After six pages of action in the mountains, the book went back 40 years to the beginning of the marriage and explained how the family came to be in such dire straits, ending with the story of how they escaped. In order to understand Susan's story, however, I needed to start by asking her about her childhood and upbringing, because only then could I understand how she would have felt upon meeting an Iraqi man and falling in love with someone from a different culture. Without knowing about her background, I wouldn't have been able to understand how she felt upon first arriving in Iraq as a young bride. Her reactions to everything she saw would have been very different if she had been there before – because her father was in the diplomatic service, for instance – and much more dramatic if she had never been abroad at all. If she had never met an Arab of any description, she would feel a much greater sense of disorientation and shock than if she were already familiar with the Muslim way of life.

In Colonel Mark Cook's book, *A Promise of Hope*, we opened with a scene that actually happened when he wasn't around, but which was crucial to his later experiences:

> All the children were asleep when the shell landed on the orphanage roof. The explosion reverberated through the thick walls, which had stood for a hundred years, providing a sanctuary and a home for many thousands of children who had nothing else in life.

After ten pages of painting the scene in Lipik we went back to Mark's life in 1992, when he first went to Croatia, and only ever touched lightly on what had happened in his life before that. But it was important for me to know about his formative years in order to understand how he would have reacted to the terrible sights he saw in Croatia when he arrived to command the British contingent of the UN Protection Force.

To understand why Donya Al-Nahi might feel so strongly about children being with their mothers that she would be willing to risk her own life and freedom by rescuing them, the reader of *Heroine of the Desert* needed to have glimpses into Donya's own childhood. The following paragraph from the book puts things into perspective and was only possible because I had asked questions about her early years:

> I really didn't enjoy my own childhood much. It makes me feel sad to say that because it should be such a wonderful time in everyone's life, but it's no good pretending. My mother and I did not have a good relationship and maybe that's why I feel so strongly that children like Leila, who have mothers that love them, should be allowed every chance at happiness. Personally, I would have been quite happy if someone had turned up to snatch me away from my family.

And to understand how a British girl would become so enmeshed in the Muslim world that she would be able to operate almost as a native in a variety of Arab countries, the reader had to see her own development, as in the following extract:

> His family home was completely different from any I'd ever known. Not just because it was a Jordanian style of house, built to keep out the heat and to be the home of an extended family, but because it was full of people who cared about one another, who spoke pleasantly and respectfully to each other. It was a completely different atmosphere from the sterile world of resentment and constant complaining, the anger and the explosions of physical punishment that I'd been used to all through my childhood. No one scolded anyone else, or talked about them behind their backs, or shouted at them. Everyone laughed and hugged and shared their emotions and their possessions. All the generations of the family ate together at mealtimes and talked to one another as equals. They were a proper, warm, loving family. If this was the Muslim life, I decided, I wanted more of it.

So, in order to understand how your author is thinking or feeling at any point in their story, you need to know what has gone before. Ask questions about their childhoods and early lives, even if they're not going to appear in the story; you need to know about them in order to understand the author and catch their voice more accurately. If they had a bad relationship with their parents then you will better understand if they have difficulties with their in-laws. If you know they have been abused or bullied in the past, then you will be able to see why they react towards certain people in later life in certain ways.

In the case of Kathy Etchingham, her childhood was crucial because it was the reason she ran away to London at the age of 16, falling in with the rock stars of the time and ending up living with Jimi Hendrix. Their troubled childhood was one of the things the couple had in common, so her book, *Through Gypsy Eyes*, opened with her as a little girl and then pretty much followed her life chronologically.

I stood at the gate every day for three weeks, waiting for my mother to come home to get us like she promised. It was eerily quiet for most of the day, since there were no other children living in our row and hardly any traffic ever passed by. It gave me plenty of time to think.

The ghostwriter may even need to know this information if someone is writing a book that is nothing to do with their own lives. If you are writing a gardening book for a television gardener, and they tell you they were brought up in a house that was surrounded by dark and threatening trees and 20-foot hedges of Leylandi, that may well be relevant to their theories on landscaping and pruning. If you're writing a management book by someone who left school at 14 with no qualifications and rose to the top through sheer hard work and entrepreneurial skills, the tone will be very different from that of another management book written by someone who went to Harvard and worked their way up the corporate ladder of major companies. To get the right voice you must know the person – and to know the person you must ask the right questions.

Sometimes an author's modesty can be a problem for a ghost. I once wrote the autobiography of an African chief who was so modest about his achievements that it wasn't until we were some way into the interviewing process that I began to understand just how important he was in his home country, and indeed in the international business community.

To get modest people to talk about themselves you have to take a firm but gentle approach, drawing them out as you would in a dinner party conversation. Be honest with them if you don't think you are getting enough material to make the book work, and tell them that you appreciate their modesty, but...! Occasionally, remind them that the book is only being written because they have achieved extraordinary things, which readers will want to know about. Make it clear that you are going to be writing in their voice and so will not put any words into their mouths that would cause them any embarrasment.

It is difficult to balance the urge to write a book about yourself with an inbuilt belief that boasting is a bad thing. A ghost needs to be conscious of any sort of dilemma that the author may be experiencing, to ensure that the final product does not make them sound unduly pleased with themselves – or indeed, as with the African chief, risk missing an important part of the story.

By the time you are ready to start the writing process you will probably feel that you have asked as many questions as you need to get the right tone and pace for the story. When you actually sit down to write it, however, you may find that there are one or two areas where you are still a bit hazy about the details. The chances are that you can clear up these questions over the phone, or at least in one more, reasonably brief meeting. Don't be shy about going back to the subject with more questions; by that time they should be feeling very at ease with talking to you and they will welcome the contact.

After the first flurry of activity at the beginning of a book project it can sometimes seem to them as if everything has gone rather quiet. However much you may have explained that you are now going to disappear for a few weeks to do the writing, they're bound to feel a sense of anticlimax and wonder what's going on. By ringing them up now and again with supplementary questions you will reassure them that the book is getting written and make them feel a part of the process.

Making the sale

Even if you've been commissioned for a ghosting project by a publisher, the editor doing the commissioning may ask you to create a synopsis or 'selling document' that he or she can use to convince and inspire others in the company – such as the sales team and the marketing and public relations departments. This editor will be as keen as you and the author to make the book a success and will need all the help you can provide. In such circumstances the synopsis probably only needs to be a couple of pages long: sales teams do not want to spend too much of their time reading lengthy documents; they want to be shown the main points, possibly in bullet form, so that they can get on with their job of convincing the bookshops to order large quantities.

If the project has been brought to you by an agent, you will be one step further away from the final publishing deal and will need to create a slightly more elaborate synopsis. If the author comes to you direct and you haven't lined up a literary agent, then the agent is the person this first document will be aimed at. Hopefully the synopsis you prepare to convince the agent will be strong enough to convince a publisher – although in some cases an agent may have suggestions as to how to improve the first draft before they send it out.

Once you have enough material (and one long meeting with the author is usually sufficient), prepare the document to make as powerful a case as possible for why the book will be a success. When you have finished, show it to the author (unless they have told you not to bother and are willing to leave the whole selling process to you). Explain to them that everything in the synopsis doesn't necessarily have to be in the book, and that there will be plenty of chances to change the tone and content at a later date. Explain that at the moment, the main objective is to get a deal and persuade a publisher to put some money on the table.

If the author is paying you a fee and is not expecting to find a publisher, then you don't have to worry about this bit.

Once the author has had their say and made whatever changes they want, you then send the synopsis to the agents or publishers that you think will be interested and settle down to wait. If you have made your approach professional enough, you should receive a reasonably speedy response compared to a first-time author, but there will still be a delay as people read what you've sent, think about it and talk to colleagues.

Hopefully, however, you will have a deal within two or three months and it will then be time to start the real writing. Sometimes I have done enough interviewing for the synopsis to be able to write the whole book without going back to talk to the author again. In most cases, however, the synopsis required one day of interviewing and it takes several more days to get enough for the final, full-length manuscript.

The weeks or months when the agent is trying to sell the project to publishers can be very difficult for the author of the book. For the ghost, the waiting is less gruelling as he or she is familiar with the routine and can be getting on with other work in the meantime; but often, the author has by this time become impatient to see the book published. Agents are not always very good at communicating with clients when they have nothing positive to report (some of them are pretty terrible even when they do), and the author is left in an uncomfortable limbo. Sometimes it falls to the ghost to keep their spirits up with a few morale-boosting phone calls assuring them that these time lapses are quite common and it doesn't mean that the book won't sell in due course.

Let the writing begin

The sale has happened; the delivery date has been set. Now, at last, you are ready to write the actual book. By the time you get to this stage you should have a pretty clear idea of the structure you want to use and the voice of the author – it's just a question of sitting down to do it.

In the very best cases, where the story has completely gripped my imagination, I find I'm able to sit down and write the bulk of it from memory. I then play through the tapes to check that I've remembered correctly and that I haven't missed out anything vital. There's nearly always something that I've forgotten and I then go through adding extra pieces into the manuscript.

In other cases the story might not be quite so gripping and I will write it in 'chunks', listening to the tapes as I go along to refresh my memory. This is where you will be deeply relieved if you have managed to persuade your author to tell their stories chronologically, or at the very least in the order in which you want to write the book. If you have to keep searching for specific passages from ten or 20 hours of tapes, you are going to end up wasting a lot of time and become deeply frustrated.

As you write, get the author's voice firmly in your head. Be sure that you can imagine them saying or writing the words that are coming out of your brain. Do not be tempted to put in jokes that *you* might find funny, but they wouldn't. At the same time, bear in mind what the reader is hearing. If the author tends to sound bitter about something that has gone wrong in their lives, you will have to temper that bitterness if it isn't going to alienate the reader, or bore them. You need to edit your subject so that they appear at their very best. They can anger the reader, but they mustn't bore them.

As well as imagining that you are speaking in your subject's voice, you also need to imagine that you are in the situations they are describing – just as you would be doing if you were writing fiction. You need to build the suspense and make the action dramatic, just as if you were writing a thriller. There must be cliffhangers and mysteries on every page to keep the reader turning over.

When I was ghosting for Tan Sri Loy, the author told me about an attempt made to kidnap him and his siblings when they were living in a jungle village. He told the story very matter-of-factly, but it was an event that could easily be dramatised with reference to previous events in the story, which I also knew about by then:

> 'Quick,' our neighbour whispered as she opened the back door so we could escape unseen. 'Run!'
>
> We fled blindly into the damp blackness, just as we had run from the Japanese all those times before, the leaves whipping our faces and the roots tripping us up as we stumbled away in tears.
>
> When we thought we had gone far enough to be safe we stopped and huddled together all night, terrified that they would hear our crying and come after us with machetes. The night seemed to last forever, a hundred times more frightening than it had ever seemed when we had been with our parents in the makeshift hut. When light finally came and we emerged cautiously onto the road, the car had gone and so had our mother.
>
> 'They took her instead of you,' our neighbour told us. 'They were very angry with your father for sending you away.'

In *My Gorilla Journey* I needed to pull together the various characters of the different animals that author Helen Attwater had encountered, and integrate them into the story of the struggles which she and her husband were having with disease and war – as shown in the following extract:

> My lap was soon a crowded place. Mayoko and Mabafi piled onto me, the latest burst of gunfire leaving them trembling, their tiny hands squeezed tight as they clung to my body. Sid's group, restricted to the cage and unable to pursue their usual daily explorations of the forest, had

climbed to the highest point of the cage and looked down at us as we sat hunched against the brick wall. As another burst of gunfire rang out, followed by the boom-boom of a mortar, they screamed, their lips drawn back in a grimace of terror. Mark moved away to enter the cage and the gorillas descended silently from its roof and were soon huddled in the refuge of his arms, gazing questioningly into his eyes.

The power of tears

Quite often, particularly if you are helping them write a memoir or autobiography, the author will dissolve into tears when they're telling the story. As I mentioned in chapter 3, many of them liken the interview process to therapy. If it is going well, they may be releasing emotions they have been keeping a tight hold of up till that moment, and going over memories that may be painful.

Your job under these circumstances is to pass the tissues, keep quiet and keep recording. If you're hoping to produce a book that is emotionally powerful and moving for the reader, the tears of the author are a very good sign. If you start crying too it will be even better.

When I was helping Beverly Peberdy write *Do Robins Cough?* I found myself frequently having to take breaks from the keyboard in order to regain my composure. Beverly was writing about her time working in the madhouses of Romania where perfectly normal, tiny children had been imprisoned for years, tied to their cots and deprived of all stimulation, until eventually they went as mad as the older inmates. One particular child had become so much part of her life that she and her husband adopted him once Beverly's time in Romania was over. We started the book with her arrival at the madhouse where she would spend the majority of her time while in the country, and, hopefully, left the reader in no doubt about how emotionally gruelling the story was going to be. The boy's eventual triumph over his appalling start in life made it one of the most uplifting tales imaginable:

The guard shuffled along with us to a pair of metal doors and unlocked them with another key-jangling performance. Once he had conquered the lock he threw open both doors in a gesture of welcome and the blast of putrid air made me step back in shock. It was like a great heat hitting us and I retched involuntarily at the smell of rotting food, urine and excrement, mixed up like some giant, steaming compost heap.

Inside everything was grey, gloomy and wet. A couple of small, shadowy figures darted across the passage from one of the rooms, pursued by the shouts of angry women. The floors and walls were all running with water and there were no windows. As the doors banged shut behind us, the key crunching in the lock, it took several moments for my eyes to adjust to the darkness and even then I was only able to see a few feet ahead. Somewhere, far down the high windowless corridor, one light bulb emitted some feeble rays. The cold and damp made me shiver but the worst thing of all was the noise. Frantic, distorted folk music blared deafeningly from invisible speakers but even that wasn't loud enough to cover the manic screaming and moaning which seemed to come from every side. It wasn't like listening to human voices; it was like a tide of misery washing over us. I felt completely lost and trapped.

One of the most powerful premises for any story is when the author has previously lived what might be described as an 'ordinary life' and is suddenly catapulted into extraordinary circumstances – either by their own choice or because of something someone has done to them. *Sold* was, I believe, as successful as it was because every female reader could imagine herself suddenly thrown into the same nightmare as Zana and Nadia Muhsen. In *Do Robins Cough?* the readers could imagine that they too had made a decision one day to go out into the world and make a difference, with the same gruelling but eventually triumphant results. Both Zana and Beverly found qualities within themselves that they never knew they had, which is always inspiring and moving for anyone to read about.

Anecdotes

It's always a joy when you have an author who's full of anecdotes, but you have to be careful that the final product doesn't
end up sounding like a joke book. Leonard Lewis, indisputably
one of the greatest hairdressers of the last century and a pivotal
figure in the 'swinging London' scene, was full of good stories
when I ghosted his autobiography *Leonard of Mayfair*, but I
needed to graft them into the narrative in order to sustain the
pace for a whole book. I opened with a chapter set in the salon
on a busy morning with several different things happening at
once. By having a number of storylines going at once it was possible then to bring in the following story – which had been told
to me by a number of different sources as well as by Leonard
himself – as if it was just part of the morning's trials and tribulations, quickly moving on at the end to another anecdote:

'Mr Leonard,' the girl cried as I put down the phone,
'come quickly, there's a slight problem.' She clattered away
on her high heels, without telling me what was happening.

I swept downstairs to find an air of barely suppressed
panic enveloping the usual calm of the reception hall.

'It's Miss Collins,' one of the receptionists whispered to
me.

'What about her?' I demanded. I had been with Joan
just a few minutes before and she had been perfectly
happy.

'She's on her way down,' the girl squeaked, 'and we got
her coat out of the cupboard to be ready ...'

'Yes?' I was getting annoyed. What could possibly be so
terrible to justify all this hysteria?

'One of the juniors hung it in a cupboard which had
fresh paint on it,' she said. 'The decorator hadn't put a sign
up. She had no idea!'

She held up the priceless coat. The tips of the fur all
down one sleeve carried a vivid white stripe where it had
brushed against the wet paint.

'What are we going to do?' the receptionist wailed. A
small crowd of employees was forming around us. 'She's
on her way down.'

'Stall her,' I barked.

Several of them scurried off to the main staircase to intercept the descending star, who was not renowned for her patience with fools. I stared at the coat for a moment, wondering what I could possibly do to remove the paint in the time it would take Joan to descend the last few steps. I knew that my good friend and accountant, Neville Shulman, would not be best pleased if I told him we were going to have to buy her a new coat. It seemed like hours, but it can only have been a matter of seconds before I knew what had to be done.

I whipped my comb and scissors out of my top pocket. At the speed of light I ran the comb down the sleeve and trimmed off the painted ends of the fur, like mowing hideously expensive grass. I had to work fast but at the same time I had to be careful not to cut too much. When I reached the top of the stripe I realised that the other sleeve now looked different. Swinging the coat round I repeated the exercise on the other side. I could hear Joan becoming irritated by the people fussing over her on the staircase, asking her if she would like a drink or coffee before she went. Her voice was clearly audible above their chatter, the ringing tones that would later make her so effective as the terrifying vamp, Alexis, in Dynasty.

'I'm in a hurry,' she announced as she tried to shoo them out of her way. 'I have a lunch appointment. Will you please fetch my coat and let me through?'

As she entered the reception area she saw that 'Mr Leonard' himself was waiting to usher her from the premises, holding out her coat. Her face softened into a beautiful smile at this obvious tribute to her importance to us as a client. I draped the mink flamboyantly over her shoulders. I whisked my fingers through her hair exclaiming at the perfection of the cut, kissed her on both cheeks and she stalked from the salon, purring happily.

Breathing a sigh of relief I returned to the first floor to see how my other clients were faring.

'I can't wake my client up,' Clifford complained as I came onto the floor.

Dialogue

Imagining how conversations might have gone and inventing dialogue can help to speed a story along. You can never be entirely sure that you have reproduced the words accurately, unless someone happened to be running a tape recorder at the time, but readers are always willing to suspend their disbelief if the dialogue is believable and seems to fit the characters.

The following is an exchange from Donya Al-Nahi's *Heroine of the Desert*, where she and a mother she was helping had managed to track the woman's children to a flat in Amman where they were hidden behind a locked front door. They knocked and the following exchange took place. Rather than reporting it second-hand in Donya's words, I put it into speech marks:

'It's Kate, the children's mother,' I called back in Arabic. 'She's come to visit Rana and Hanan.'

'Go away!' the woman shouted. Her voice sounded frightened but I couldn't tell if she was frightened for us or for herself. 'Go away now!'

'We don't want to cause any trouble,' I assured her. 'Kate just wants to visit the girls.'

'You can't come in here,' she shouted back. 'Go now or I'll call the police.'

'Mummy, Mummy!' a small girl's voice rang out, but was quickly muffled, as if someone had put a hand over her mouth.'

'Rana?' Kate screamed. 'Rana, is that you?'

I thought that by using this device, the scene would become much more alive and immediate. In *A Promise to Nadia*, Zana Muhsen's second book, a group of mercenaries offered Zana their services to get her sister, Nadia, out of the Yemen by force. Again, I thought the use of dialogue would help to dramatise the situation and explain why Zana was so convinced by the men's arguments and willing to pay them an enormous sum of money in advance:

'We'll lift them out by helicopter,' Don explained. 'We've found the best position for the chopper to be waiting, so we can get to it quickly and be away before the men know what has hit them. And we need to have a ship ready to fly everyone out to.'

'Where will the ship be waiting?' I wanted to know.

He spread the map out again and pointed to the southernmost point of the Red Sea, where Yemen almost reached across to Africa.

'There,' he said, 'in Djibouti. It's a French-speaking port, the major one for the Gulf of Aden. It's Ethiopia's main outlet to the sea.'

'Good,' I said, 'if it's French that's all the better. The French government have done more to try to help us than anyone else.'

'We want to go in during Ramadan,' Don said, 'when everyone is fasting and sleeping during the day. That way they will be less alert and there will be fewer men out and about. By the time they've woken up to what is going on we will already be in the air.'

The first draft

The aim is to make the first draft as close to perfect as possible – partly because you don't want to alarm the author by showing them a half-finished product, and partly because it is quicker to get things right first time rather than having to do re-writes when you should be getting on with your next book. When you employ builders to do major work on your house, there is a long period when the place looks like a bomb has hit it and you can't believe order will ever be restored. Then suddenly the final effect comes into sight and you feel a sense of overwhelming relief. That is the feeling you want to engender in your clients, without the worry about the early mess. You don't want them to see the first chapter until it is as good as it can be, which isn't likely to happen until you have finished the whole draft, doing all the polishing and correcting that you need to do.

It may be that you are working on more than one project simultaneously; doing synopses for future books and editing past books at the same time as you are writing the bulk of your current project. The financial realities of the market mean that you can't always dedicate the whole of your attention to one book at a time – otherwise there would be long gaps after each one was finished while you tried to get another one going. Try, however, to spend large chunks of every working day on the main project when it is at the first draft stage, until you have got the majority of it written. It will take much longer to finish if you keep breaking off for a few days or weeks and then have to get yourself back into the frame of mind you were in when you were last working on it.

I always find that the hardest part of the process is getting the first half of the words out onto paper. It feels rather like being a sculptor confronted with a ten-foot high block of stone. Once you've chiselled it into roughly the shape of your life-sized sculpture, putting in the final touches becomes a pleasure. The daunting bit is at the beginning when you still have to conjure up 80,000 or 100,000 words out of nowhere.

Although you probably won't start work on the first draft until you feel you have a complete grasp of the story and the author's voice, you may find that when you have actually poured the story out onto paper it isn't as long as you thought it was going to be, or that there are gaps in your knowledge you didn't notice when you were doing the initial interviewing. If you feel brave enough, you could show the author this first rough draft, although it would be preferable just to have a list of questions prepared that would fill in the gaps. You may find, for instance, that they described an incident to you in a few words and, being anxious not to interrupt their flow, you neglected to ask them to elaborate with enough detail to make it work on the page. Once you have seen how the book is working it will be reasonably easy to get them to fill in the gaps for you during one or two more days of interviewing. You will then be able to finish the first draft.

Presenting to the client

It may be that you are still a few thousand words short of the final target length when you finish the first draft. It is perfectly reasonable to show the typescript to the author in this state, as the chances are they will have suggestions for extra material to go in. But handing over the actual manuscript is always a nerve-racking moment. What if they hate it, after all that work? I have to admit that this does happen on occasion ... but if you've had a good rapport with your subject and you've done your homework, it's unlikely.

The first draft should be shown to *no one* until the author has okayed it: they have final veto on what should and shouldn't be in it – because only if they're confident that they have the ultimate say will they be completely open and honest with you during the interviews. The ghost can advise and recommend, but the author has the last word. If there is arguing to be done, let it be done by the agent and the publisher.

Sometimes the author is immediately thrilled with the manuscript, brimming with praise for the way in which you, the ghost, have climbed inside their heads. But not always and there is a good reason for this.

You know how it is when you are at a party and someone snaps a Polaroid of you with your mouth wide open, laughing uproariously at someone's joke? When they show you the picture you go, 'Oh my God, rip it up, I look terrible!' The reason you think that is because it isn't the expression you normally put on when you know someone is taking your picture. After a few moments, however, you look at it again, and you can see that it is actually rather a fun picture. You might not like the look of yourself with your mouth wide open and your eyes screwed up, but you do look as if you're having fun. It's a natural, happy picture. After a few days, when you come across it again in your pocket, you actually rather like it and prop it up in pride of place on the mantelpiece. It's a good picture because it's a true picture of what you look like and it captures the mood of how you were feeling at the moment it was taken.

If you, as a ghostwriter, have done a good job of the manuscript, you may find you get a similar reaction from the author. Because you have written things that they think and have said to you, but might not choose to say when they're on their best behaviour, they may throw up their hands in horror, saying, 'I can't say that!' or 'I don't sound like that!'

The important thing is not to panic. Tell them there is no need to worry, all they have to do is make whatever changes they want on the manuscript pages and you will incorporate those changes in the next draft, before anyone else sees it. Don't become defensive of your work, because then an argument will ensue, you will both get into fixed positions and there will be no chance of finding a middle road.

Give them the manuscript and a coloured pen or pencil and tell them to get editing. When they actually sit down and try to think of better ways of saying things, if you have done a good job of capturing their true thoughts and feelings, they won't be able to.

What often happens next is that they ring and say they have made a lot of changes and that you need to meet up to discuss them. Once again, resist all urges to panic. When you get there you will almost certainly find that they have changed virtually nothing. They may have made one or two small corrections on each page, which will look like a lot at first glance, but actually won't take you more than a few hours to incorporate. In most cases, when you hand the manuscript back with the revisions they will be thrilled, especially as they will feel they've contributed to the writing process with their suggestions and corrections. It's like the tale of the instant cake mixes, which housewives initially refused to buy until the marketing people thought of telling them to add an egg to the mixture, even though it wasn't needed. The customers immediately felt less guilty about using an instant mix and felt themselves to be part of the cooking process. Sales soared as a result of this simple device. Always be happy to allow the author to add their egg into the editorial mix.

If they still aren't happy with the book and you are not sure what else you can do to change it, you might suggest that you send a copy to the agent for their opinion. With any luck the agent will either like whatever you have written and will help you to allay the author's fears, or they will have suggestions on how you can change it to make them happier.

I have probably been involved in around 50 ghosted projects at the time of writing this book, and out of those, only two had to be abandoned because the author was too unhappy with the book to want to continue. It's very depressing when it happens, but then there isn't a profession in the world where you can guarantee to make a hundred per cent of your customers happy. The best hairdressers in the world have days when clients burst into tears when they see the final results in the mirror, and the finest lawyers in practice sometimes fail to get their clients acquitted and still have to be paid. If you have done all the right things and given it your best efforts, you can't do more.

If the relationship does break down in this way, it is then helpful to have a mutual agent who is friendly to both sides and can broker some sort of financial deal which will make everyone feel reasonably satisfied. You then just have to be philosophical and get on with the next project, which will undoubtedly be a roaring success.

The author takes over

Once the author and the publisher are happy with the manuscript, your work is more or less done. You may be asked to read the galley proofs when they come back from the typesetters, or to provide an introduction or an epilogue. The publisher may also ask you to pen some copy to go on the cover, since you're the person who knows the book and the author better than anyone.

Whether you own a share of the book or not, it is in your interests to help market it in any way you can – since the more successful the book is, the more useful it will be in bringing more work your way. Always agree to do whatever they ask for: these jobs never take long.

I have had authors who have asked me to go along with them to talk to sales conferences or to sit in with them on media interviews, but they are in the minority and they tend to be people who think of the project more as a collaborative book than as a ghosted one. I am always pleased to help in any way I can, since it gives me a chance to see the other parts of the publishing process in action and to meet people to whom I might be able to sell other projects at a later date. In most cases, however, the ghost hands over the manuscript and the author and publisher take over from there. If you own a share of the book the agent will ring you occasionally with good news about some serialisation or film deal or foreign sale; you and the author may exchange the odd phone call or Christmas card, but your lives tend then to drift apart.

A surprising number of authors, once they have enjoyed a success with their first book, will be eager to repeat the process. They sometimes think that next time they'll be able to do it themselves and then find that when they actually sit down at the desk it is no easier than it was when they were trying to create the first book on their own. Several of the people I have ghosted for in the past have come back to me for second books, and sometimes even third or fourth ones. When that happens, and the bond of mutual trust has already been established, the process becomes far more straightforward.

Expect no glory

A ghost must expect no glory. Enjoy the experience of researching, writing and being paid to do pleasant work. Sometimes your name will get mentioned on the cover of a book and sometimes it will appear only on the flyleaf. Sometimes you will get a mention in the acknowledgements and sometimes you will not appear at all. You may get billed as 'co-author', but 'By Big Shot with Joe Bloggs' or 'as told to Joe Bloggs' is more likely. It's always useful to have your name there, but it can never be allowed to become a problem if it disappears.

If you hear the author talking on chat shows about how hard the writing process was, just be glad that they are getting the opportunity to promote the book, and proud that you did such a good job they now actually believe they wrote it themselves.

These are the main stages of the ghosting process:

Make initial contact with the author and ascertain if theirs is a story that will sell to a publisher and that will hold your interest during the writing process.

Be firm but kind in turning down projects that you do not want to do.

Help to sell a project if it hasn't yet got a publisher.

Find a location that your subject will be most comfortable in when interviewed.

Make sure your recording equipment is as discreet as possible.

Ask every question that the reader is going to want to know the answer to.

Dramatise as much as possible, without overdoing it.

Blend anecdotes into the story.

Don't be afraid of tears – theirs, yours or the readers'.

Encourage the author to make any corrections, additions or deletions that they wish in the draft text.

Once you have handed the book over, forget about it and move on to the next project.

Expect no glory.

10

Ghosting Fiction

There are a number of different situations in which a ghost might be asked to create a work of fiction that they will not have their name attached to in more than a subsidiary role.

There are the 'celebrity' books, which purport to be written by someone famous but are actually little more than merchandising exercises.

There are the 'blockbuster' novelists such as Tom Clancy, who are known for a certain type of fiction and come up with plots (or authorise ones that other people have come up with) that will be written by someone else and go out primarily under the famous author's name, but with the collaborator's name in smaller print below.

There are the novelisations of television series or films.

There are the book series, which go out under a fictitious name and are written by a string of ghosts. The latter are most often found in the children and teenagers' book market, since children show an enormous loyalty to brands of books. Once they've enjoyed one they like to see the same formula repeated over and over again, whether it is about ponies or ghosts, vets or Californian high schools.

All these types of books are generally commissioned from the ghosts by the publishers. Deals are struck and the ghosts know exactly how much they will be paid and how much credit they can hope to receive, if any.

Then there are the speculative projects where someone with an idea for a novel (or their agent) approaches a ghost and suggests a collaboration. Here, there is no money on the table until the book has been sold to a publisher. Now, writing fiction is fun – but selling it is a complete nightmare. Every day I receive at least one phone call from someone who has a great idea for a novel; one which all their friends tell them is bound to be a bestseller and which will also make a blockbuster of a movie. Very often their ideas *are* excellent ... but unfortunately, having an idea for a great story is the easiest part of the operation. Writing it is a little harder, and persuading a publisher to buy it is almost impossible.

I have written fiction of my own (including a book about a ghostwriter, called *Maisie's Amazing Maids*) and I have ghosted fiction, but there has always been a good reason why the risk has been worth taking. The idea either came from a celebrity and so the publishers knew how they would market it, or it was so strong that it had already been commissioned by a publisher who then had to find a writer to produce the goods. Being asked to ghost fiction, and being paid for it, doesn't happen very often – but when it does, it is well worth doing.

Dramatising true stories

The other thing that would-be authors often say is that they don't want to write their life story as 'fact' because of legal or personal complications, but would like to 'turn it into a novel'. What they don't realise is that in turning their story into fiction they're removing half of its saleability. As a non-fiction title the publishers would at least have had a marketing handle; as fiction, it's just one more made-up story amongst thousands of others that come out every year.

There are, however, exceptions to that rule and there are some stories that lend themselves well to dramatisation. *The Disappearing Duke*, the synopsis of which appeared in chapter 8, is one good example. There were a lot of areas in the story where it was hard to get the necessary proof, and a great many long and tedious court cases. If we had written it as a straight factual account the book would have been a very heavy read and would only have been of interest to a small number of historians. By dramatising it, rather as one would for a movie, Tom Freeman-Keel and I were able to make it a more interesting and informative read. The opening scene, for instance, ran as follows:

> The gravediggers saw her coming but kept their eyes cast down on their shovels, hoping the one-woman hurricane

just might be diverted off course before she reached them. But Mrs Anna Maria Druce was not about to be diverted by anybody. Her eyes were entirely fixed on the bent backs of the men as they laboured in their parallel graves in the earth. It was June 1898.

They knew who she was. Not because they'd read about her in the papers, although their bosses at the London Cemetery Company had most certainly been following Anna Maria's exploits with exceptional interest, but because they'd grown used to seeing her at the cemetery every day, accompanied by a man who looked as if he was a professional of some sort – an expert, a man who might be consulted on matters of some importance.

Although I knew from Tom Freeman-Keel's research that Anna Maria Druce had made a nuisance of herself in the graveyard, and that she had been an angry, driven woman, I didn't know if a scene like this actually happened between her and some gravediggers. It didn't matter because the point was to illustrate her state of mind and the situation she was in as quickly as possible, catching the readers' attention and making them want to know more.

Similarly, when I was approached by a self-confessed gangster called Norman Johnson to write his autobiography, we found it hard to convince a publisher that Norman's story was sufficiently different from other gangsters' to merit an advance large enough to support us both through the writing period. Part of his story, however, was about an incident where he accidentally found himself working as an armed guard for a Middle Eastern princess when he was one of the most wanted men in England. He and the princess subsequently fell in love. It was an unusual love story and one of the publishers we sent the initial synopsis to suggested we wrote that part up as a novel. We accepted the challenge and the book was subsequently published under the title *The Princess and the Villain*. The action on the first page opened in the year 1970:

'I'm getting married, Norm,' Len said, obviously nervous.

'What? To that?' Norman jerked his head in the direction of the woman sitting next to his brother. It wasn't that she was ugly or anything, actually she was in pretty good condition for a woman of her age. She certainly looked after herself. The figure was trim and the hair expensively cut. There was a lot of jewellery on her. She obviously had money.

The biggest difficulty with these sorts of dramatisations is that the bookshops aren't quite sure how to categorise them. Even though the publisher was behind the idea of *The Princess and the Villain*, the book didn't do as well as we all felt it deserved and that seemed to be because the bookshops weren't sure what department to put it in. Was it a novel or an autobiography? Should it be under crime, romance or general? As a result it fell between every stool and failed to find a market. That is one of the reasons why it is so hard to fictionalise true stories.

Perfect plots

Now and again someone will approach me who has worked out a brilliant plot for a novel and has either had a go at writing it and not been happy with the results, or else knows they will never get round to it and wants me to do it for them. If I have really liked the story and felt that there was a strong chance the book would find a publisher, I have agreed to undertake the job. Sometimes I have charged them a fee and sometimes I have agreed to work for a percentage. Sometimes we have been successful and sometimes we haven't.

If someone comes to you with the perfect plot and you believe you can make it into a bestseller, by all means have a go. But know that you will almost certainly have to write the whole thing on spec before a publisher will make an offer. Publishers won't pay until they have seen more or less the whole book, unless there is a very big name attached to it which they know will guarantee a certain level of sales. The chances of success for a first timer are about on a par with the national lottery – but then if you don't buy a ticket from time to time, you have no chance of winning at all, do you?

The odds of finding success with any fictional work are always heavily stacked against you; not because you're a bad writer or because your co-writer has thought up a dud plot, but just because it is the toughest market in the world – well almost the toughest. Writing original movie-scripts on spec might just be worse (and I suspect that earning a living from poetry is no bed of roses either).

Working together

Collaborating with someone on a fictional project can be a great deal more difficult than with non-fiction. Everyone has different pictures in their imaginations and one or other partner will have to compromise at some stage if agreements are to be reached. You need to lay out the rules for the division of labour at the beginning if you aren't going to drive one another mad. If they've created a plot and you're doing the writing, then you need to run any changes of plot and character that you want to make past them before forging ahead, and you have to have as clear an idea of what they are envisaging as they do. In some cases they will have only the fuzziest idea of what they want, leaving you plenty of leeway to develop your own ideas; but if they have already developed pictures of the characters in their heads they will be uncomfortable with you messing around with them.

The best way to work is to take the project in stages. Start with a synopsis of the story that you are both agreed on. Then agree on the characters and a chapter breakdown. When you are both completely confident that you are working to the same template, then you can start to write the whole book.

Unlike non-fiction, where I would always advise the ghost to try to write the whole first draft before showing it to the subject (see pp. 125–8), with fiction it is probably better to take it a chapter or two at a time to ensure that you are both still travelling along the same lines.

If the subject believes they can write as well as you and are only using your services because they don't have the time to do the job themselves, then you may find them interfering with your prose. If you haven't laid down the rules at the beginning then you are going to have to put up with this. Remember that they are ultimately the boss and you are the ghost. If they truly hate a character you have created, then you will have to 'kill him or her off'. There will not usually be room for two muses in one project. Listen carefully to their suggestions, explain clearly why you disagree with them if you do, but be ready to give in if they are insistent. Remember, this was their baby first; they gave birth to it, you are just helping them to bring it up.

You will be able to gauge pretty early in the process whether or not you are going to be able to work together peacefully. If you aren't, then there will have to be a very good financial incentive for continuing with the struggle.

The ground rules for ghosting fiction:

Be aware that fiction is far harder to sell than non-fiction.

Be open to suggestions for fictionalising true stories.

Make sure that the demarcation lines of editorial responsibility are clearly drawn.

Be sure you will be comfortable working with your co-writer.

Take it in manageable stages.

11

The Necessary Skills

In earlier chapters of this book, I covered why you might, or might not, wish to become a ghostwriter – and why people might be likely to seek out your skills. But just what skills *does* a ghost need? What qualities are likely to make the difference between success in a rewarding profession, and a realisation that in fact, ghosting isn't for you?

An ability to suppress your ego

Ghosts must suppress their own egos completely – a good discipline for any writer, but an essential one for ghosting. As a ghost, you're fulfilling a similar function to that of a barrister in court – using your skills to plead the case of your client. Authors need ghosts who will not challenge them, but will simply listen to what they have to say and understand why they did what they did. If the ghost wishes to be critical of the subject then they must step back and create an objective biography, not an autobiography.

This is the author's book, both in their own eyes and in the eyes of the publishers and eventual customers. A ghost must have no expectation of receiving any praise or glory whatsoever for the job. If the book goes ahead and is published and sells well, then that is reward enough, and other thanks or praise must come as an unexpected bonus. If you are going to be the least bit upset not to see your name credited or not to be invited to the launch party then you are going to have a miserable time ghosting altogether. (You usually will be invited to the launch party – just don't count on it!)

It is essential for the ghost to make the subject feel completely comfortable in his or her company. If they think they are going to be criticised, judged or argued with, the authors will not relax, open up or talk honestly. It's not the ghost's job to try to make them change their opinions about anything or anyone, but rather to encourage them to tell their story in the most interesting and coherent way possible.

The book is not a platform for the ghost to air their own views on anything at all, unless those views coincide with the author's.

The ability to see a structure

When a subject first approaches a ghost, they are usually highly anxious to get their story across. Quite often they have a grievance against someone who has done them wrong, or an enormous enthusiasm for some project that they want to write about. As a result of their enthusiasm they tend to pour everything into the first telephone call, or even the first meeting. They tend *not* to be good at working out what the most interesting and important points of the story are, which is one of the reasons why they need a ghost in the first place.

The second skill you need, therefore, is the ability to look through the outpouring of detail and the jumble of facts and opinions and see what the basic premise of the book might be. As the relationship develops, you then have to be able to see the structure of the story in a way that will support a book. What is the central theme? Where should the story start and end? How should it be paced? Which parts of the information that is being poured out are relevant and which are irrelevant? What help is the reader going to need in order to follow the story and understand the important points?

These are the questions that will determine the basic structure of the book. Without them you will just have an 80,000-word stream of consciousness, which may work if your name is James Joyce (although there are some who will argue it doesn't even work for him), but probably won't work if you are a battered wife or a gangster, an abused child or a groupie to the stars. So a ghost needs to be able to see the possible outline of the story almost from the beginning, to know what questions to ask and which bits of the story to ignore. Only in this way can you present the project to publishers in an attractive and saleable form.

During the actual writing of the book, the ghost also needs to be able to see a structure – in their mind's eye, or else mapped out on sheets of paper if that helps – in order to write it effectively.

When Zana Muhsen thought about her life over the previous ten years, for instance, she saw a continuous stream of terrible events, all bleeding together in her mind into a catalogue of worry and unhappiness. In order to turn those years into a story (which became the book, *Sold*), there needed to be a beginning, a middle and an end – and plenty of tension along the way. The beginning of the story, therefore, was when her father suggested that she and her sister, Nadia, go to Yemen for a holiday. The tension was the discovery that they had been married off to strangers and were to become virtual prisoners in an alien world. The reader needed to be simultaneously horrified and fascinated by the things she had to tell, and to be gripped by the adventure of the girls trying to escape back to England. The end of the story came with Zana's final escape, leaving behind both Nadia and the son that she had borne in her forced marriage. The dynamics of the story conform perfectly to the rules that a teacher of creative writing might suggest for pacing a novel, but Zana herself was far too close to the detail to be able to see that structure for herself, being more intent on railing against her father and the other men who had caused her misery.

Similarly, Donya Al-Nahi's life is a hectic round of adventures, stakeouts and car chases, dashing from one country to another rescuing children in dangerous circumstances and then escaping across international borders, often on forged papers. At the time we wrote the book *Heroine of the Desert*, she had undertaken about a dozen of these missions, but simply describing them one after another would have become repetitive for the reader. Once again we needed to find a structure, starting with the first woman who approached her for help and ending with a disaster in Dubai where she was captured and imprisoned with the mother she was trying to help. The reader is therefore taken on a journey that gradually becomes more and more exciting and dangerous as it progresses, hopefully holding their attention from start to finish. As the plots unravelled we were also able to intersperse it with insights into Donya's past, many of which were startling adventures in themselves, and which added to the reader's understanding of her character and of what drove her to take the risks that she did.

An ability to ask the right questions

Ghosts don't need to be experts in everything they write about, but they need to understand enough about a subject to be able to ask the right questions. If you truly can't think what to ask an author then the chances of the partnership working are nil. You need to be as anxious to get to the truth as the potential future reader.

A ghost must never be afraid to admit their ignorance to their author, and whenever they do so they will be pushing him or her to explain themselves still more clearly. This will help both the ghost and the eventual reader to understand the story and the person who is narrating it.

In some cases it might even be a good idea to pretend to know even less than you actually do, because by asking questions you are forcing the author to think through exactly what the truth is and making them express it in their own words – words that you want to be able to use in the final manuscript.

If, for instance, you are dealing with someone who has been kidnapped in a third-world country and taken to a hideout somewhere in the mountains, they might tell you that 'it was horrible', but you need to know more. If you have been to that country, you might be able to fill in the gaps with your own description, but you might not see this place in the same way as the author. So you need to coax them to describe it further.

'Horrible how?' you might ask.

'Well, it stank,' they might say.

'Stank of what?'

'Cow dung.'

'Why?'

'Because they kept their cattle downstairs at night, and the walls were made of this paste which was half cow dung and half mud. It was okay at night when it was cold, but during the day, when the sun was up, the smell was overpowering.'

'How did you find all this out?'

'I could hear the cows moving about below us at night. I was really scared at first, till I realised what it was, and I saw the man next door building an extra room on his house through a crack in the wall. I could see the mixture he was using.'

With the answers to these obvious questions you have enough material to build a really powerful couple of paragraphs, whereas before you had only three words – 'it was horrible' – which didn't paint any sort of picture at all.

Seeing things through another's eyes

It's crucial that you don't start seeing the story through your own eyes – either by speaking in your own voice, or by inserting facts that you may know but the author almost certainly would not. When I was writing about Zana Muhsen's adventures in Yemen, for instance, I was aware that when she was taken to Aden on a visit I could have inserted a few paragraphs about the political history of the place and its connections to Britain. But if I had, it would have completely wrecked the illusion that the story was being told by a 15-year-old girl. At that stage Zana was only interested in the immediate dangers and fears that assailed her. She was obsessed with how she and her sister were going to escape from the clutches of the families that had virtually enslaved them, and only worried about the heat and exhaustion and the cruelty of her daily life. She knew nothing about the history of Aden, and cared even less. Before writing anything at all, the ghost must be sure that they can imagine the words coming from the mouth of their subject.

Listening and not judging

Ghosts have to love to listen to other people talking. The only time you need to talk is when you want to put your subject more at ease, or when you are guiding them with questions as described above. You need to have infinite patience to allow people to rant and rave if they want to, and even to talk complete nonsense now and then. And then you steer them back onto the path that you need. Sometimes your attention will wander, which is why you need to have a tape running as well (see chapter 9), but you still have to be able to resist the urge to speak instead of listen.

Just as a ghost needs to suppress their ego with regard to getting credited on the cover of the book, they also need to suppress the urge to voice their opinions and to argue with the subject. If you are ghosting the autobiography of an assassin, for example, there is a strong chance that you will disagree with the way in which they rationalise their profession to themselves and to other people. They will take for granted certain moral assumptions that most people would find unacceptable. Your job as a ghost is *not* to show them the error of their ways; you are not a priest trying to redeem their lost souls. Once again, you are more like their lawyer; someone who listens to their case and then pleads it on their behalf in terms more eloquent than they themselves could manage.

If, when your assassin tells you how he blew the head off some South American dissenter, you throw up your hands in horror and tell him what a bad man he is, he will immediately become defensive and will stop being open and honest just when you want him to tell you more, not less. You don't have to tell him you approve of his chosen method of earning a living; you don't have to tell him anything at all. You just have to keep asking the questions that will shed light on why he has chosen that way of life, how it works and what it feels like. Perhaps there was something in his childhood or early adulthood that hardened him to killing. Or some part of his make-up that is 'missing'. You need to be able to winkle the essence of his thinking – or possibly lack of thinking – out of him so that you can portray it for the rest of the world to read and reach their own conclusions.

If the subject's life is too distasteful for you to be able to allow them to speak unchallenged, then you probably aren't the right ghost for that job. You don't have to like the subject in order to ghost for them successfully, although it certainly makes the process more enjoyable if you do, but you do need to be interested in them and want to find out more. You will only find out more if you ask the right questions and listen very carefully to the answers, win their confidence and encourage them to be themselves and speak as they would if they were amongst like-minded friends. If they sense that you don't like them or don't approve of their way of life they will clam up and you will never get a satisfactory book out of them.

Half the job of ghosting is about finding out about other people. The other half is turning what you find out into words. If you aren't interested in anyone but yourself then at least half of the process is going to be an agony. When you meet people for the first time, do you want to know everything about their lives? Do you want to know what they have done and what they have seen? Do you want to learn everything possible from them?

If the answers to those questions are yes, then you will enjoy being a ghost.

Being trustworthy

Subjects need to be able to trust their ghosts completely. You can start that process off by signing confidentiality agreements (see pp. 54–5), but hopefully once the relationship is underway they will be able to tell that you will never treat them dishonourably. They need to know that you will keep your word on everything. If you say you will do something for them then you must do it; if you promise a deadline, then stick to it.

In some cases *they* may let *you* down. They may mess about with appointment times or they may tell you things that aren't strictly true. You are not allowed the same luxury. If they don't trust you to do what you say, then they won't be able to trust you not to steal their words and sell them somewhere else. If they're famous they'll be worried you might talk to the tabloids, or they may worry that you will take their story and turn it into a novel of your own. You must have the same sort of professional credibility as a lawyer, a doctor or an accountant (I know you can point to bad eggs in all these baskets, but you get my point). The subject's role is to be colourful and interesting, which may involve also being a touch unreliable or economic with the truth. Your role is to be the solid, reliable part of the relationship.

Make them absolutely aware at the start of the relationship that no one else will read anything you have written for them until they have seen it first. Assure them that you will always make the changes they ask for. Explain that you might point out why you thought it would be better to do it another way, but if they definitely want to make a change then they have the final say. Stick to your word. Once they're confident that you are trustworthy, they will relax and give you a far better insight into their lives and thoughts and souls.

An ability to write in other voices

One of the problems of persuading new clients to hire you as a ghost is that they tend to ask to see something else you have written. If the potential client is a middle-aged, public-school-educated general, and the only book you have to show him is the story of a 16-year-old girl pop singer from the back streets of Glasgow, he's likely to feel uneasy. He will read the book and see that it is a million miles from the voice he would want to use. He will see words and phrases that he probably doesn't even understand, let alone use. As a result he will probably look for another ghostwriter – one who has dealt with generals, or at least colonels, before.

What the ghost has to get across to anyone who will listen is that the voice in any given book they've written is not their own. If you were a playwright and you created a play with a number and variety of different characters, no one would expect you to have them all speaking in the same voice. Nor would they expect the characters to have the same views on life – as each other, or as their creator. In fact, if they did, you would have a play with virtually no credibility or dramatic tension whatsoever (unless it was a monologue, of course).

A ghosted book is like a long monologue in the voice of a character. You have to be able to put yourself inside the skin of the author and write as if they were the ones with their fingers on the keyboard. It is a skill a little akin to acting. Your thoughts and experiences have to be translated into their words and seen from their perspective. If you can only write in one voice then you are going to have to find clients who talk and think in that voice. The resulting market is likely to be very limited – although there are writers who do succeed by specialising in military books, for example, or books about film actors of a certain age. If you can think like people of different genders, ages, backgrounds and even nationalities, ghosting is going to prove a very rewarding experience.

Skills a ghost needs to have:

An ability to suppress their ego.

An ability to see the structure of a story from among seemingly random material.

The ability to ask the right questions.

The ability to see the world through other eyes.

The ability to listen and not to judge, and to be interested in other people.

Trustworthiness.

An ability to write in other voices.

12

Helping Authors Self-Publish

When most authors get as far as talking to a ghostwriter, they're usually hoping to sell their book to an established publisher (or have already done so). They are expecting to receive an advance payment, the prestige of a famous imprint and then all the support of an established distribution and marketing system.

The ghost, too, is hoping to find authors who will meet with this degree of success – and many do. Sometimes they achieve it with the help of the ghost and sometimes they are able to arrange it for themselves. Anyone who has ever tried to sell a book project to publishers, however, will know that it is one of the toughest markets imaginable. Many good stories and worthy books never manage to find a publisher who is willing to put money into backing them. When that happens the author has to decide whether to abandon their hopes for publication, or whether they should try to find an alternative way through the maze.

There is a great, and justified, fear amongst writers of falling into the clutches of organisations known as 'vanity publishers'. For anyone who has not come across them, these are firms who will publish books for authors if the author is willing to pay all the costs. This in itself is a perfectly respectable thing to do, but less scrupulous operators will lure that author into the deal with flattery. They will tell him or her that they are certain the book will find a market and earn back far more money than the few thousand they are being asked to lay out for its printing and production. When they make these promises, they are almost always being economical with the truth. If the book had that great a potential in the first place then one of the other, more established firms would already have made an offer. If the author swallows the bait, they may well end up with a consignment of handsomely bound and printed copies of their book but will receive no further assistance in marketing or sales. This is not a desirable state of affairs and should be avoided. That does not mean, however, that authors have to abandon all hope of publishing themselves in a realistic and satisfying way. In order to keep a project alive when there is little chance of an established publisher making an offer, and to make at least some of the author's dreams come true, the ghost can offer some alternatives.

Find out what they truly want to achieve

Right at the start of the process, find out what the authors want to achieve – apart from realising some vague dream of writing a bestseller. It may be that a management-training guru wants a book that he can sell to candidates who come on his courses, as well as one that will promote his name in bookshops and in the book-review sections of the business press. If he tells you that he thinks he can sell two or three thousand books himself, then a publisher might well be willing to put the book out under their imprint on the understanding that the author will buy the first two thousand copies of the print run at a wholesale price. That way the publishers know that their costs are covered and that any extra sales that happen through the shops or other market-ing outlets will immediately bring the project into profit. The author may not have been paid a huge advance, but he will be able to sell the books with the same mark-up as the bookshops in order to make a profit on the two thousand copies he has bought, which will defray the cost of hiring the ghost, and will have achieved his objectives – of getting his book into the shops, and raising his profile with potential customers as well as those who come on the courses. Once the book is in existence, and the costs are recouped, both the author and publisher would be able to concentrate on finding other ways to promote and sell it.

The prospect of organising all this might seem daunting to a busy management trainer, but if the ghost offers to approach publishers on his behalf with the suggestion of the deal and a synopsis of the book, the chances are he will be happy to hand the project over. The ghost will benefit by making it possible to finance the writing of the book and by getting to talk to a selec-tion of publishers who might want to use his or her services again; the author gets his book published and may even make a profit; while the publisher gets a title with almost no risk attached.

Another would-be author might be an elderly lady who wishes to record her life for the benefit of her family. She may or may not expect it to be bought by a publisher. If there is no chance of any major company taking it up, there is still no reason why she shouldn't have it self-published, provided that she is fully in the picture about how much it will cost and how it will not generate any income for her. There are now any number of companies that advertise their ability to produce small print runs and it doesn't take too much research to find one that would suit the needs of any ghost's client.

Doing the research

Many of the companies who provide these sorts of services are listed in *Writers' and Artists' Yearbook*, and a lot advertise in the various writing magazines that you can buy in newsagents such as *Writers' News* and *Writers' Forum*.

You can either compile a list of numbers for your author to call, or make the contact yourself as part of the ghosting service. Prices will vary enormously, as will the potential quality of the finished product. The biggest influence on price will be the number of copies to be printed: a few dozen may cost almost as much as a few thousand from some larger printers, whereas specialised, print-on-demand firms will be able to produce very small numbers at economic prices. The market is changing all the time and each project requires new research if the best deal is to be sniffed out.

To assess the integrity of a publishing company, ask to see other books they have created and maybe even for a couple of names of satisfied customers you can talk to. The best way to judge, though, is by using your gut instinct. Do you like the person you will be dealing with? Have they made any foolish, inflated promises about being able to 'market' the book for the author? None of them can do that.

Protect them from false promises

If you have a hand in finding the publishing services your author needs, you can help make sure they're not falling prey to false promises. Make them aware that unless they have a way of selling the books themselves (like the management trainer in the example above), then they have to expect not to recoup any money from the project at all. They are simply commissioning a book as they might commission a family portrait or a piece of made-to-measure furniture. If they then manage to sell some copies, or a large publisher sees the self-published volume and makes an offer, all well and good – but this is not to be relied upon.

What self-publishing authors must realise:

Anyone who promises to sell lots of copies for them is making promises they can't keep.

If they hope to recoup some or all of their outlay they must have a captive market to sell to.

If they want to commission a self-published book with no means of controlling sales themselves, they must look on it as a luxury they are buying for themselves and not a business opportunity.

13

Summing Up – the Happy Ending

Because I am so enthusiastic about the ghostwriting profession, I may have given the impression that it is an easy way to make a living. If so, then I should qualify my words just a little with a warning.

If it is a path that you decide to follow, you will be beset by many obstacles along the way. There will be the people who manage to infect you with their enthusiasm for their story to such a degree that your sense of judgement is temporarily derailed and you end up spending weeks on a manuscript that has as much chance of taking off as a firework in soup.

There will be the SAS officers who are revealed to be skilful fantasists – but not until the books you wrote for them, telling of their daring exploits, are riding high in the charts and the investigative journalists start poking around.

There will be the famous clients who think nothing of telling you they will meet you in New York and then manage to be in Paris at the designated time, having completely forgotten to inform you of their changes in plan.

There will be the subjects who tell you that they don't like what you've written for them but can't quite put their finger on why that should be, giving you absolutely no clue as to what you should be doing differently.

There will be the publishers who leave their companies just after commissioning your book, only to be replaced by others who have no interest in your subject whatsoever. There are also some highly distinguished publishers who seem to be completely unable to market the books they have commissioned and manage to aggravate celebrity authors to such an extent that the celebrities start phoning you in the middle of the night with their complaints about not being able to find their books in Harrods and not having their phone calls to the publishers returned.

If you can just keep going through these trials and tribulations, you will find that every so often you stumble into a project which travels on oiled wheels. You will meet a subject who truly inspires you with renewed faith in mankind, and you will occasionally produce a bestseller that has the publishers filling the high streets with dump bins, display racks and cardboard cut-outs of the author.

When you have been working as a ghost for a few years you will be able to gaze on a shelf-full of books with different authors' names on the spines, knowing that without your input they would never have existed, and you will be able to look back on many encounters with extraordinary and varied people. Despite all the frustrations and annoyances you are going to be facing, it is still a wonderful way to spend your life.

Just to end, may I crave one further indulgence from you patient readers who have stayed the course, and quote a short sequence from my novel *Maisie's Amazing Maids*? I believe it sums up the heady mix of highs, lows and infinite variety that make up the life of the ghost ... The scene is a barbeque at the house of a gangster whom Joe has been ghosting for:

'So you're a ghostwriter, then,' a man tearing into a spare rib said. 'Who you writing for now you've finished Len?'

'Well,' Joe hated these sorts of conversations. He preferred asking questions to answering them. 'I've got a few projects in the pipeline.'

'Like who?' His interrogator obviously didn't intend to let him off the hook.

'Well, Marion Ray is thinking of doing a book...'

'Oh yeah? I like her. She's what I call a real star,' another face announced, biting into a hamburger, the bloody sauce dripping unwiped down the parched riverbeds of his scarred chin.

'And I've been approached by a Filipino girl who seems to have been brought over here as some sort of sex slave.'

Index